daybook, *n.* a book in which the events of the day are recorded; *specif.* a journal or diary

DAYBOOK

of Critical Reading and Writing

D1317054

AUTHOR

VICKI SPANDEL

CONSULTING AUTHORS

RUTH NATHAN

LAURA ROBB

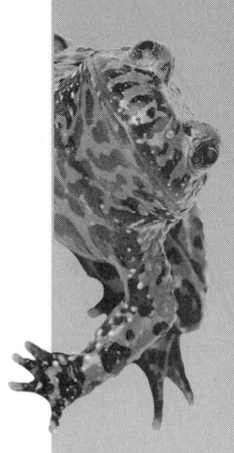

Great Source Education Group
a Houghton Mifflin Company
Wilmington, Massachusetts

Author

VICKI SPANDEL, director of Write Traits, provides training to writing teachers both nationally and internationally. A former teacher and journalist, Vicki is author of more than twenty books, including the new third edition of *Creating Writers.*

Consulting Authors

RUTH NATHAN, one of the authors of *Writers Express* and *Write Away,* is the author of many professional books and articles on literacy. She currently teaches in third grade as well as consults with numerous schools and organizations on reading.

LAURA ROBB, author of *Reading Strategies That Work* and *Teaching Reading in Middle School,* has taught language arts at Powhatan School in Boyce, Virginia, for more than thirty years. She also mentors and coaches teachers in Virginia public schools and speaks at conferences throughout the country.

Printed in the United States of America

International Standard Book Number: 0-669-48040-1

5 6 7 8 9 10 - PO - 09 08 07 06 05

R e a d e r s

Great Source wishes to acknowledge the many insights and improvements made to the Daybooks *thanks to the work of the following teachers and educators.*

Madeline Andrews
North Londonderry Elementary School
Londonderry, New Hampshire

Linda Cooper
North Londonderry Elementary School
Londonderry, New Hampshire

Janel de Boer
Stonewall Elementary School
Nicholas, Kentucky

Candy Hernandez
Dike-Newell Elementary School
Bath, Maine

Judy Hughes
Panama City, Florida

Cindy Hutchins
Fisher Mitchell Elementary School
Bath, Maine

Liz Johnson
Lincoln Elementary School
Mount Vernon, Washington

Lois Johnson
Cedar Grove Elementary School
Panama City, Florida

Deb Larson
Berryton Elementary School
Berryton, Kansas

Emily Luke
Patronis Elementary School
Panama City, Florida

Judith P. McAllister
Fisher Mitchell Elementary School
Bath, Maine

Arlene Moore
Lincoln Elementary School
Mount Vernon, Washington

Cathy Paquette
Dike-Newell Elementary School
Bath, Maine

Kim Prater
Cedar Grove Elementary School
Panama City, Florida

Barbara Pringle
South Elementary School
Londonderry, New Hampshire

Patty Roberts
Mark Twain Elementary School
Littleton, Colorado

Beth Schmar
Emporia State University
Emporia, Kansas

Jean Smith
Depaul University
Chicago, Illinois

Lucy Smith
Patronis Elementary School
Panama City, Florida

Table of Contents

Table of Contents (continued)

Pupil's Skills and Strategies

LESSON TITLE	LITERATURE	AUTHOR	RESPONSE STRATEGY	CRITICAL READING SKILL
Unit 1: Reading Well				
Getting the Big Picture	from *Why Do We Laugh?*	Ann Redpath	ask questions	main idea
Reading into a Story	from *Sarah, Plain and Tall*	Patricia MacLachlan	mark up the text (clarify)	inference
Thinking Ahead	"Hare, Otter, Monkey, and Badger"	Josepha Sherman	highlight	predict
Unit 2: Reading Fiction				
Who's Telling the Story?	from *Later, Gator*	Laurence Yep	predict	point of view
Where Does the Story Take Place?	from *Charlotte's Web*	E. B. White	visualize	setting
What Happens?	"A Pet"	Cynthia Rylant	predict	plot
Unit 3: Understanding Language				
Creating Pictures with Words	from *Cookcamp*	Gary Paulsen	visualize	descriptive language
Comparing One Thing to Another	"Dreams," "Black Is Beautiful," "Black Ancestors"	Langston Hughes, Andreya Renee Allen, and Brandon N. Johnson	highlight	figurative language
Stretching the Truth	from *Davy Crockett*	Mary Pope Osborne	mark up the text (clarify)	figurative language
Unit 4: Reading Authors: Roald Dahl				
A World of Make-Believe	from *The BFG*	Roald Dahl	ask questions	fantasy
Writing for Laughs	from *The Twits*	Roald Dahl	highlight	humor
Picturing a Magical Place	from *Charlie and the Chocolate Factory*	Roald Dahl	visualize	descriptive language
Unit 5: Reading Well				
Alike and Different	from *Throw Your Tooth on the Roof*	Selby B. Beeler	ask questions	compare and contrast
Asking Why	from *And Then What Happened, Paul Revere?*	Jean Fritz	highlight	cause and effect
Time Order	from *One Day in the Prairie*	Jean Craighead George	mark up the text (clarify)	sequence
Unit 6: Reading Nonfiction				
Skim First	from *The Kid's Guide to Money*	Steve Otfinoski	ask questions	skim and scan
Tell It Like It Is	from *Avalanche*	Stephen Kramer	highlight	summarize
Using Graphic Aids	"Settling the Midwest"		highlight	using graphic organizers

WRITING	FOCUS
main idea paragraph	To find main ideas, look for the author's most important points about the subject.
double-entry journal	Use the information the author provides to make inferences about characters' feelings and situations.
rewrite story ending	Making predictions about what will happen next keeps you involved in a story.
rewrite a scene	Point of view in a story affects how you "see" events and characters.
description of a special place	When you read a description of a setting, form a picture of the place in your mind.
plot sketch	In many stories, the plot centers around problems and how they end up or are resolved.
descriptive paragraph	When you read descriptive words and details, try to picture the character or scene in your mind.
poem with figurative language	When you read a metaphor, think about how the two things being compared are alike or what the comparison suggests.
plan a tall tale	As you read, notice the way authors use similes or exaggeration to emphasize an idea or to add humor.
journal entry	Part of the fun in reading comes from sharing in the author's wild imaginings.
opinion paragraph	Authors use humor to entertain readers.
descriptive paragraph	Writers use descriptive language to create pictures in the minds of readers.
interview	To compare, ask yourself: How are these things alike? How are they different?
journal entry	When you read about a series of events, look for causes and effects, or events that bring about other events.
step-by-step paragraph	As you read, look for sequence words to help you keep track of the order of events.
create a poster	Skimming and scanning before you read can help you learn what the selection is about.
summary paragraph	When you summarize a story or article, you tell only the most important ideas.
fill in a graphic organizer	Graphic aids help you understand what you read and keep track of what you've learned.

WRITING	FOCUS
rewrite with synonyms	Sometimes the best part of a story or poem is the words the writer uses.
diary from pet's point of view	Personification is when a writer gives an idea, object, or animal human qualities.
onomatopoeia poem	Writers use onomatopoeia to engage the reader's "sense of sound."
word picture	As you read, try to compare yourself to a character and imagine yourself in the same situation.
character sketch	Pay attention to a story's characters. Think about how they act and how they feel about themselves and others.
most embarrassing moment paragraph	When you read, try to make a connection between the story and your own life.
magazine article	When you read, look for the most important idea. This is the author's main idea.
double-entry log	When you draw conclusions, you think about what you know from the text and what you know from your own life.
paragraph with facts and opinions	When you read nonfiction, think about which statements are facts and which are opinions.
write a poem	Poems can bring out different feelings in readers.
word picture	Poets use words to paint pictures in the readers' minds.
write a poem using rhyme	Read poems aloud to hear the rhythm and rhyme.
context clue web	Look for clues in nearby words and sentences to help you figure out unfamiliar words.
dialogue	Authors use dialogue to move the story forward and to reveal who a character really is.
write a poem using sensory language	Sensory language makes the writer's world seem real.
write a lesson learned in a folktale	Folktales entertain us and teach a lesson at the same time.
use theme in a new folktale	In folktales, you can often discover the theme by looking at the lessons the characters learn.
journal entry	Connecting to the experiences or feelings of characters helps us to understand them.

Correlation to Writers Express, © 2000

Daybook Lesson	Writing Activity	Writers Express, ©2000
Reading Well		
1. Getting the Big Picture	write a paragraph	75-79, 82-85
2. Reading into a Story	write a journal entry	135-136
3. Thinking Ahead	write ending for story	45, 59, 110
Reading Fiction		
1. Who's Telling the Story?	rewrite last scene of story	45, 110, 220-225
2. Where Does the Story Take Place?	descriptive paragraph	76-78, 82-83, 127
3. What Happens?	create plot for story, with problem and solution`	35-38, 45, 47-53, 278
Understanding Language		
1. Creating Pictures with Words	descriptive paragraph including sensory details	78, 124-125
2. Comparing One Thing to Another	write short poem	239-249
3. Stretching the Truth	write similes and hyperbole	125, 127
Reading Authors		
1. A World of Make-Believe	write fantasy, a descriptive paragraph	76-78, 100-102, 105, 212-214
2. Writing for Laughs	explain opinion	76-77, 81-83
3. Picturing a Magical Place	write descriptive paragraph	76-78, 82-83, 127
Reading Well		
1. Alike and Different	interview and compare responses	159
2. Asking Why	write journal entry	135-136
3. Time Order	write descriptive paragraph using transition words	76-78, 80, 82-85
Reading Nonfiction		
1. Skim First	create a poster	
2. Tell It Like It Is	write one-paragraph summary	185-187
3. Using Graphic Aids	use given chart to organize information	

Correlation to Writers Express, © *2 0 0 0*

Daybook Lesson	Writing Activity	*Writers Express,* ©2000
Understanding Language		
1. The Power of Words	rewrite part of story, replacing underlined words with new words	292, 305
2. Is It Human?	write diary entry	135-136
3. Onomato-*what?*	write poem	239-249
Reading Authors		
1. That Could Be Me!	draw a word picture	152-155
2. Thinking About Character	write one-paragraph character description	152-155
3. Making Connections	write narrative paragraph	76-77, 79
Reading Well		
1. Is It Important?	write article for kids' magazine	192-203
2. It's Up to You	respond to quotations with personal thoughts and feelings	
3. Is That a Fact?	write informative paragraph	76-78, 80, 82-83
Reading Poetry		
1. What Does It Mean?	write short poem	239-249
2. Word Pictures	create a word picture	75-79, 82-85
3. Rhythm and Rhyme	write short poem	239-249
Understanding Language		
1. Word Clues	use context clues to find meaning of word	289
2. Dialogue Is More Than Talk	write a dialogue	215, 236
3. Use Your Senses	write sensory poem	83, 127, 239-249
Reading Authors		
1. Folktalkes: Part of a Tradition	continue writing a story	45, 58-59
2. Getting to the Heart of It	write a short folktale	8-22, 220-225
3. Understanding Characters	describe experiences and feelings	76-78, 82-85

Overview

What is a *Daybook*? Why do I need one? How do I use it? These questions come up almost immediately among teachers when they first see a *Daybook*.

Purpose

A *Daybook* is a keepable, journal-like book designed to improve students' reading and writing. Its purpose is to engage students in brief, integrated reading and writing activities daily or at least weekly. By asking students regularly to read good literature and write about it, students will become better readers and writers.

Lessons

Each lesson is a brief, highly focused activity that concentrates on one aspect of critical reading. By focusing on a single skill, students can see how to do critical reading. The lessons include models showing how to respond actively to literature in the Response Notes. Each *Daybook* even begins with an introductory "Active Reading" unit to show students some of the ways to respond actively to literature. Then, in the lessons, students respond creatively to the literature through writing descriptions, journal entries, narrative paragraphs, and many other kinds of writing—all in response to great literature.

Literature

The literature included in this *Daybook* came from suggestions teachers made. More than sixty master teachers recommended their favorite books and authors, and from these came the quality selections included here. Each selection was reviewed for its appropriateness and for its illustration of the critical reading skill at the heart of the lesson. In addition, a blend of traditional and non-traditional authors, fiction and nonfiction, and different genre were considered. At each step, teachers from the appropriate grade level commented upon the literature, readability, appropriateness of the activities, and critical reading skill.

Goals

The final result can be seen in the *Daybook*, where each individual lesson has been crafted to fit in the reading and writing curricula of elementary teachers. The goals of the *Daybook* are reflected in the headings of the units:
- to teach students how to read actively.
- to build the essential skills (such as fiction and finding the main idea) for reading well
- to develop an appreciation for the elements of fiction, poetry, and nonfiction
- to create a love and appreciation of language
- to introduce students to and foster an appreciation of fine authors and great literature

Uses for *Daybooks*

Teachers suggested numerous ways to use the *Daybook*, from introducing author studies to reinforcing key reading and writing skills. It can serve as a portfolio of daily reading and writing practice or as a guide to introducing key skills. How you use the *Daybook* ultimately depends upon you. The *Daybook* can become for you a powerful tool to help create better, more confident readers and writers.

Who Is This Book For?

The immediate response to the question "Who is this book for?" is that the audience is average, ordinary students. The *Daybook* targets everyday students in grades 3-5—neither the best nor the worst, just average students.

What's Average?

The question about the audience for the *Daybook* comes up when considering how the literature was chosen, how its readability was gauged, what assignments were chosen, and how much readiness or scaffolding is needed in each lesson. But even average students vary widely and respond much differently to individual lessons.

For example, in "Tell It Like It Is" in grade 4, students read "Avalanche" by Stephen Kramer. For students in predominately warm climates, avalanches do not represent everyday experience. Teachers there will need to build some readiness about how these occur. In one state, students may be tested on writing descriptive paragraphs in the state assessment exams, and thus practice writing descriptions regularly; but, in another state, descriptive paragraphs may just be starting to be introduced. To establish what would work on average, then, state standards as well as the appropriate on-grade-level texts were referenced. (Writing assignments, for example, were matched to expectations in such appropriate grade-level texts as *Write on Track*, *Writers Express*, and so forth. The same is true of the reading skills.) Current practices and materials provided reference points to check assumptions about what's average.

Why Use These Authors?

Likewise, selecting specific authors to feature at specific grade levels seems somewhat arbitrary. What makes Julius Lester a fourth-grade author and Patricia McKissack a third-grade one? Here teachers guided the selection of which literature and which authors to use. Asking sixty master teachers to recommend literature and authors hardly approaches scientific reliability, but it is a useful touchstone. The intent is not to limit authors or a piece of literature to a specific grade level as much as it is to offer a rich, broad variety of literature at each grade level.

What's the Readability?

For teachers in the elementary grades, helping students find materials at their specific reading level is a major challenge. Each student is different, and the right reading level for one student poses insuperable challenges for the next student. The readability of selections in the *Daybook* will change from lesson to lesson. The entire notion of "readability level" depends, among other elements, on word choice, sentence length and complexity, and subject matter. As in the case of the "Great Crystal Bear," such words as *polar, winter solstice*, and *winter* may have different levels of familiarity to students who live in different parts of the world. Readability can vary from student to student.

If one selection seems too easy or too hard for your students, realize that the selections and "readability" change throughout the *Daybook*. Lessons are organized by the critical reading skills taught, not by the reading "level" of the selection.

How Will I Know?

Is this *Daybook* right for my students? As teachers, you routinely ask this question—about the *Daybook* and all of the other books in your classroom. You want assurance that the selections will match the reading abilities of your students. One obvious answer is simply to try some lessons with your students. The experience of other teachers has been that those who get started and work through some lessons with students find a way to make the fit between the materials and the students. Each lesson in this *Teacher's Guide* includes a Vocabulary Activity and a Prereading Activity to improve students' readiness for the selection. Such supporting activities can help students with more challenging selections.

In the end, the best guide will be your own experience and instincts as a teacher. Try a number of lessons with students. Encourage them, challenge them, and evaluate them. Let your students be your guide in whether or not the *Daybook* helps and challenges them.

How to Use the Daybook

The *Daybook* is a tool. Like any tool, such as a hammer or screwdriver, the *Daybook* can have one purpose or many, depending on the ingenuity of the user. Teachers who reviewed the *Daybook* lessons suggested any number of ways they would use them.

1. In the Reading Period

Reviewers of the *Daybook*s often introduced *Daybook* lessons to students during part of their reading period. Whether they were using thematically linked trade books or anthologies, teachers saw the *Daybook*s' focused lessons as helpful ways to reinforce (or introduce) key skills and bring more good literature into their classrooms.

*Daybook*s also served as ways to kick off author studies or a series of reading skills lessons. Other teachers preferred to introduce an author or a skill, such as prediction, on their own and then complement their lessons with ones from the *Daybook*.

2. In the Language Arts Period

Because each lesson begins with great literature, teachers liked launching writing activities with *Daybook* lessons. Each lesson gives students literature to which they respond as well as a series of scaffolded assignments to help students get ready to write. Because the *Daybook* includes so many strong writing assignments (summaries, descriptive paragraphs, narrative paragraphs, journal entries, and so on), teachers like the clear, efficient ways the *Daybook* draws students into writing. The daily writing in the *Daybook*s appealed to many reviewers facing state tests, because their students would be able to practice regularly and build confidence as writers before test day.

3. In Reading and Writing Workshops

Numerous teachers use reading and writing workshops each week in their classrooms, and they found the integrated nature of the *Daybook* lessons to be a perfect fit for what they were trying to accomplish. The goals of their workshops and the *Daybook* lessons matched up almost exactly. Each lesson leads students from literature directly into writing, helping students to see the connections between what they read and what they write.

4. In Alternative Settings

As after-school tutorials and summer sessions become more common, teachers are looking for ways to reinforce key reading and writing skills. The brief, efficient lessons in the *Daybook*s fit well with the brief sessions in after-school and summer school programs. Teachers also pick and choose among the lessons in these alternative settings, focusing on areas where students need the greatest help. Here the flexibility of individual lessons that integrate reading and writing becomes valuable, because each lesson weaves together so many elements: fine literature, active reading, critical reading skills, and creative writing.

The uses of the *Daybook*s are limited only by the teachers using them. Laura Robb's article "Ten Ways to Effectively Use *Daybooks*" on pages 26–28 suggests a number of additional ways to use *Daybook*s. But, however you choose to use them, keep in mind that the original intent behind the *Daybook*s was to create a flexible tool for teachers to help them give students meaningful reading and writing activities, day after day, in their classrooms.

Frequently Asked Questions

Reviewers raised a number of questions during the development of the *Daybook* manuscript that might be useful to teachers using the series for the first time.

1. Why is it called a *Daybook*?

A *Daybook* traditionally is "a book in which daily transactions are recorded," but nowadays it is being used to mean "a journal." The name connotes "daily work," which is the intent behind the *Daybook*, as well as the idea of "journal," because a *Daybook* does become a place where students can record their work and ideas.

2. Can students write in the *Daybooks?*

Absolutely! In fact, that is the purpose behind this format. By writing in the book— their book—students begin to "own" the book. It records their work and their ideas. It becomes a personal record of their creative efforts, a portfolio of sorts of their development as readers and writers. One of the strongest elements of the *Daybooks* comes in allowing students to mark in the text, highlighting, underscoring, circling, and writing notes. Reading and writing in the same book creates the seamless integration that makes the *Daybook* work.

3. Can I photocopy these pages?

No, photocopying the pages in the *Daybook* is prohibited. It violates copyright laws that protect the authors' rights to their work and the publishers' rights to the product. Besides, the effect of working on a few loose-leaf sheets of paper or of working in a *Daybook* of one's own is very different. So, not only is copying unlawful, but it fails as a teaching practice.

4. Can I skip around, picking and choosing the lessons?

Yes, you can pick and choose the lessons you want to teach. One strong feature of the *Daybook* is its incredible flexibility, making it a perfect tool for teachers who want to interweave *Daybook* lessons into a crowded language arts or reading class period. The lessons in the *Daybook* have been organized into units with a logic and continuity that make sense; but other organizations of the lessons or individual lessons may well fit better with the specific needs of your classroom, and you should feel free to take advantage of the *Daybooks* lessons' flexibility.

5. What if my students are not active readers and need more help in learning how to mark up a text?

Begin with the Active Reading unit that introduces students to the most common ways of marking up a text. That's the obvious starting point, but it's only a start. Not every child will, in a few quick lessons, "get it." That's what the *Daybook* is for. Through repeated practice, students will "get it" and learn how to become active readers.

6. How were the literature selections chosen?

First, we asked approximately sixty master teachers what sort of literature they wanted to see, and they listed their favorite authors. With that background, the individual selections were evaluated on several criteria—the author, interest and accessibility of the selection, fit with the critical reading skill and writing skill, and overall balance of genre, sex, race, and ethnicity. But, first and foremost, the mandate from reviewers was good literature by good authors, and that ultimately guided selection of every piece.

7. How do I assess students' work?

Assessment looms as an issue for almost any classroom practice, including the *Daybooks*. How you "grade" them is an individual decision. Most teachers who have used *Daybooks* at the upper grades collect them periodically and mark in them. They may make an encouraging comment, check off that work was completed, and acknowledge the hard work and creativity students have poured into their *Daybooks*. Vicki Spandel addresses this issue of assessment more thoroughly in an article in this *Teacher's Guide* on pages 29–31. The important issue is that you assess students as active readers and as writers and that you take into account that students' writings in the *Daybooks* are responses to literature more than finished, published compositions.

Organization of the Daybooks

The units and lessons follow an organization designed to offer you the greatest flexibility in using the *Daybooks*.

Unit Organization

Throughout the *Daybooks*, three or four lessons are organized into a unit. This gives you a concentration of lessons on a general idea. For example, Reading Fiction allows you to introduce all of the key skills (plot, setting, characters) at one time. The units are focused on a few broad areas:

Introduction: Active Reading
- introduces the fundamentals of marking up texts, such as highlighting, underlining, questioning, predicting, and visualizing

Reading Well
- looks at basic reading skills, such as prediction, main idea, and making inferences

Reading Fiction or Nonfiction
- focuses on reading related to a genre, such as sequence, setting, characters, and so forth

Understanding Language
- highlights appreciation of words, sensory images, similes, and metaphors, with a focus on poetry

Reading Authors
- studies individual authors, their ideas, and skills related to their fiction

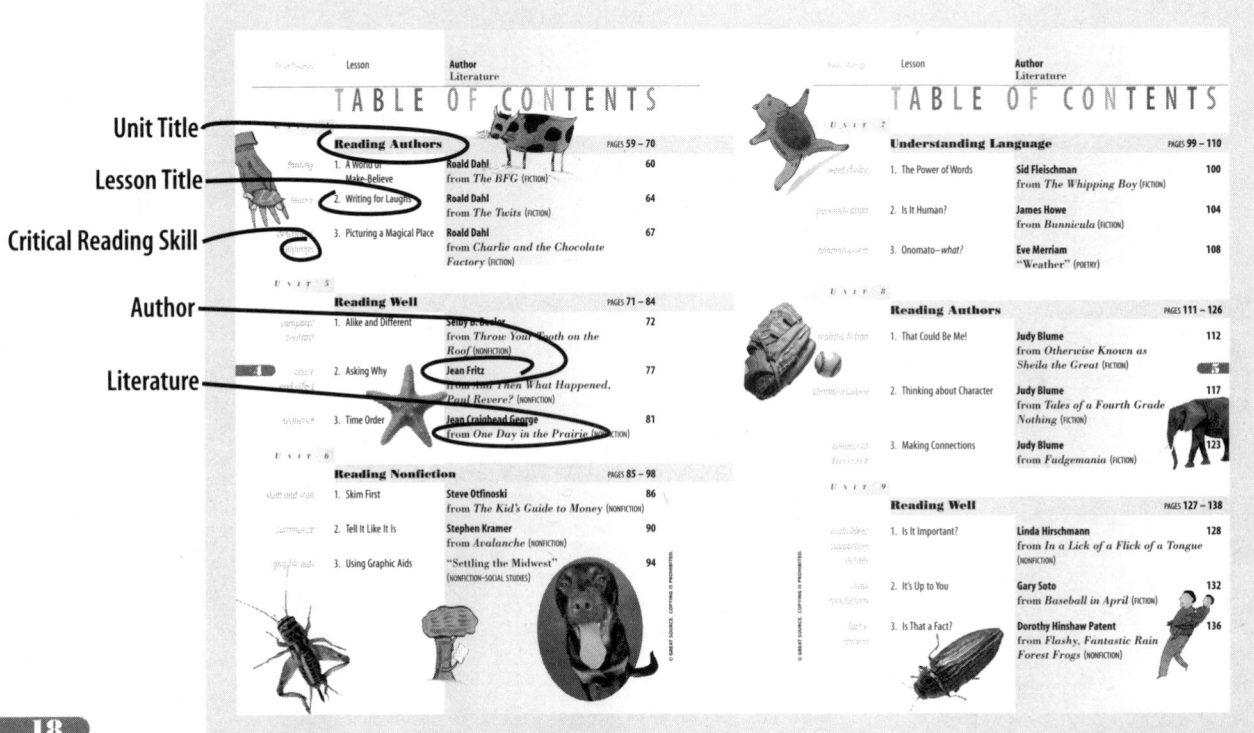

Lesson Organization

Each lesson also follows a simple, flexible organization. A typical lesson begins with a few sentences that introduce a critical reading skill. Just before reading the selection, the lesson gives the response strategy that tells students what to look for and how to mark up the text in the Response Notes as active readers. The "response" strategies given here pick up the active reading strategies introduced in the first unit, **Introduction: Active Reading.**

The literature selection follows, after which—in most cases—students have an initial activity that invites them simply to respond to the selection. This initial activity asks for their thoughts, feelings, or first impressions. Then one or more activities prepare students to write a longer assignment.

focus on critical reading

initial "response" activity

running head with unit title

lesson title

"response" or active reading strategy

Response Notes for commenting on the selection

structured activity preparing students to write

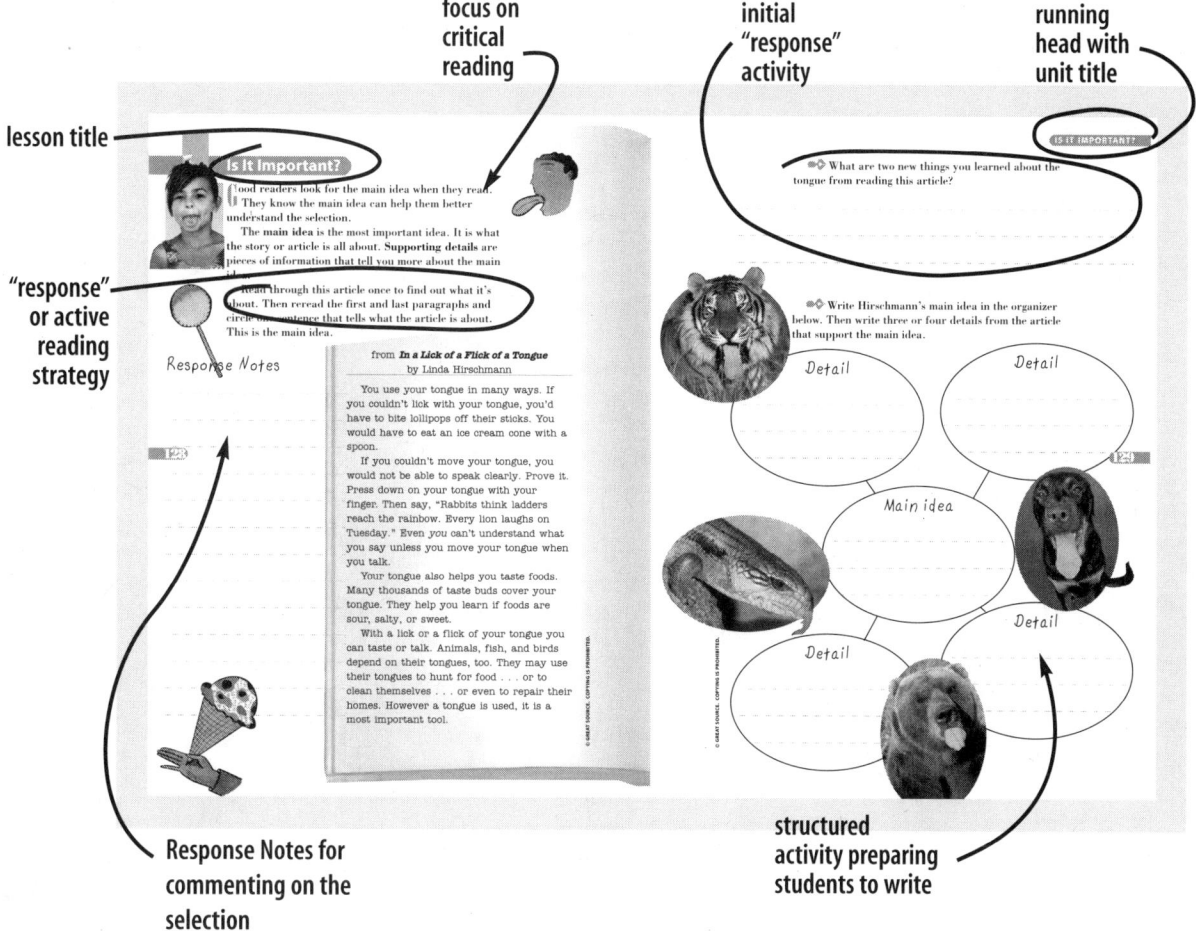

The last writing activity culminates the lesson and asks for a writing product, such as a descriptive paragraph, summary, review, character sketch, or the like. The lesson then ends with a summary statement that restates the critical reading idea.

culminating writing activity

IS IT IMPORTANT?

Write an article about your topic. Imagine that your article is going to be published in a kids' magazine. Put your main idea in your opening sentence. Then support your main idea with two or three details.

When you read, look for the most important idea. This is the author's main idea.

focus or summary statement at the end of the lesson

Teacher's Guide

Because of a strong emphasis on reading, the *Daybook* Teacher's Guide includes more than just resources for each lesson. Teachers encouraged the authors to offer more help in improving reading instruction in the classroom, and the Daybooks attempt to do that in several ways:

Program Resources
- Skills and Strategies overview
- Correlation to *Writers Express*

Professional Articles
- Ruth Nathan on "Building Better Readers"
- Laura Robb on "Ten Ways to Effectively Use the *Daybooks*"
- Vicki Spandel on "Assessment of Writing—Some Guidelines"

Reading Workshop
- workshop on key reading skills and strategies
- do-it-yourself blackline masters to implement the strategies

Lesson Resources
- prereading, vocabulary, critical reading, response, and rereading skills and strategies for each lesson
- prewriting and writing activities for each lesson

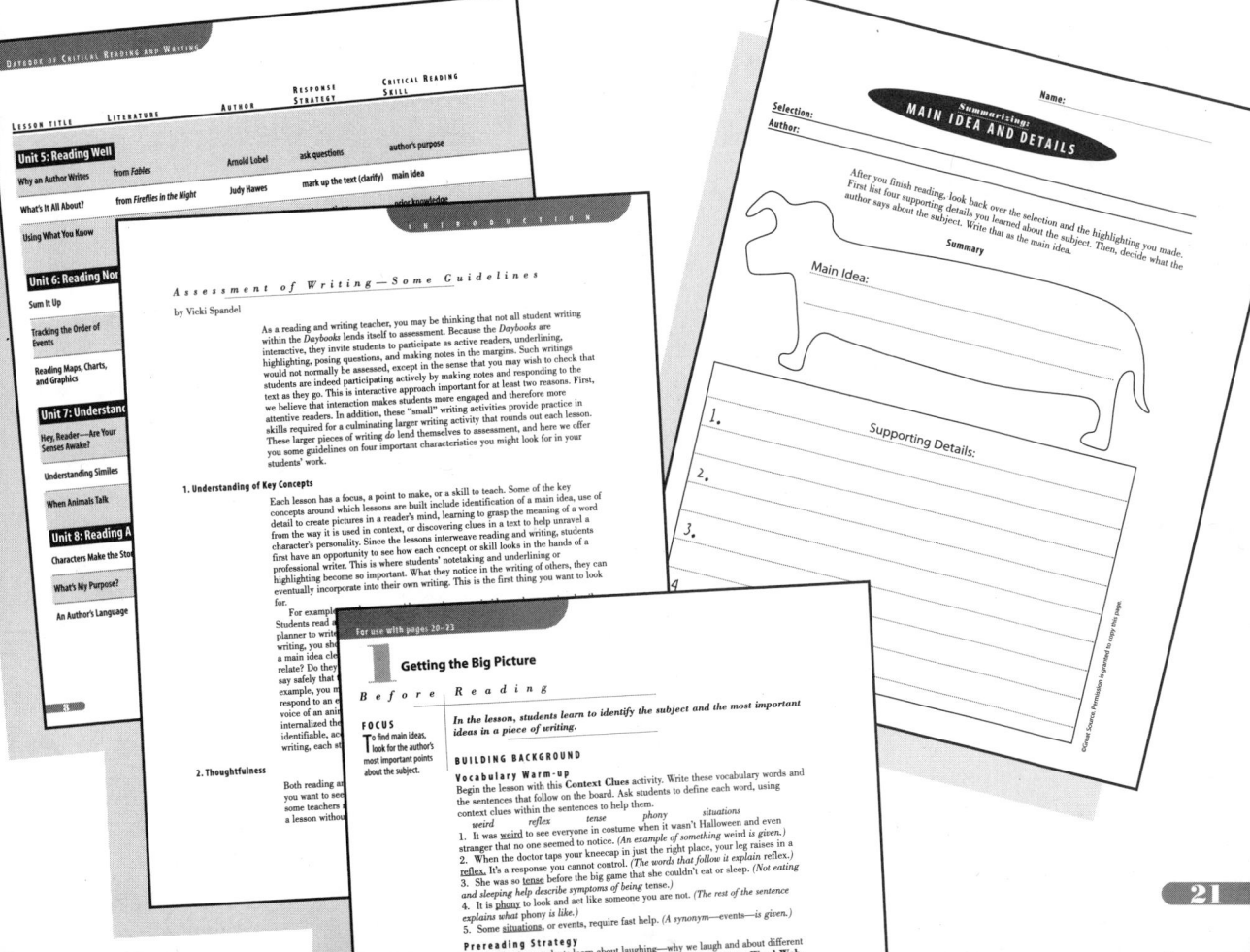

Lesson Resources

The first part of each lesson in the *Teacher's Guide* helps briefly to prepare students for the selection, providing background and introducing new or difficult words. Then each lesson discusses the response strategy, critical reading skill, and a rereading suggestion.

Focus Statement

Vocabulary Warm-up introduces new words in the selection.

Prereading Strategy builds background and readiness for the selection.

Model for active reading shown

Main critical reading focus taught and explained

Rereading Strategy encourages students go back into the selection and improve comprehension.

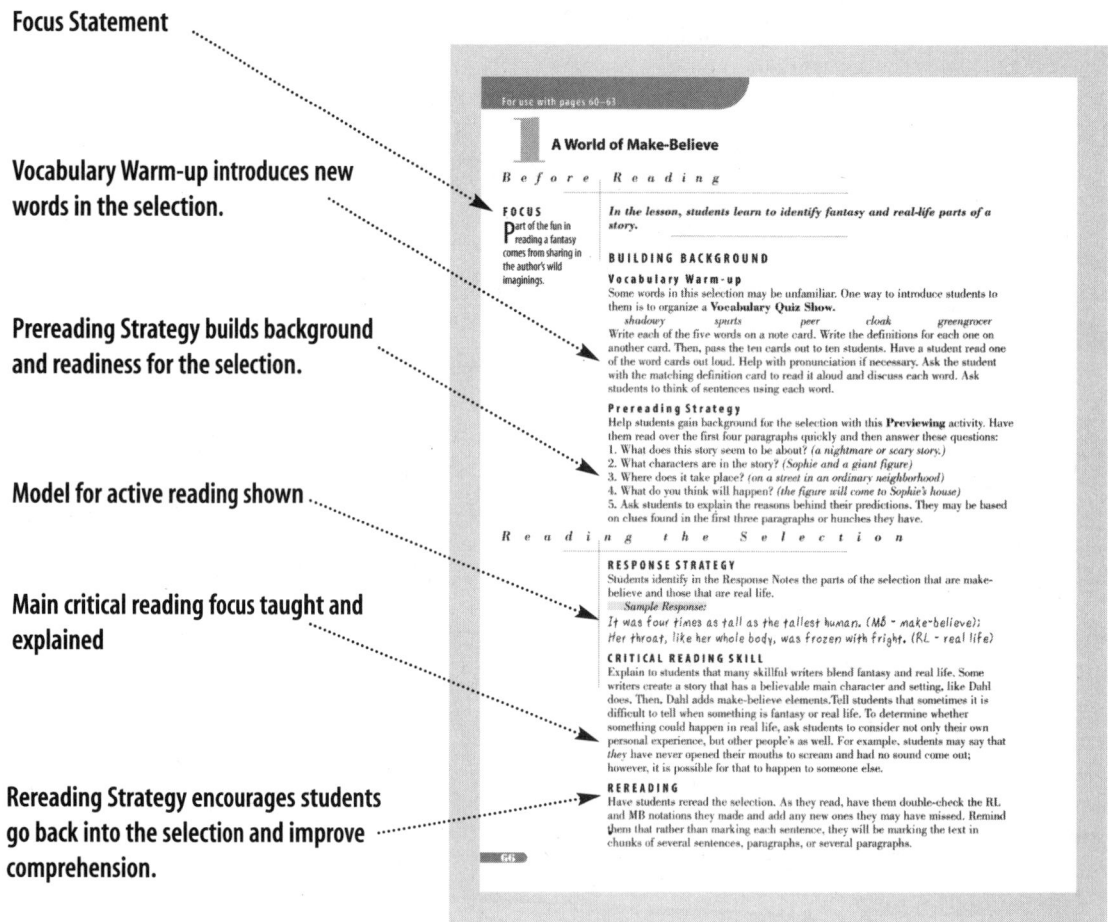

For use with pages 60–63

A World of Make-Believe

Before Reading

FOCUS
Part of the fun in reading a fantasy comes from sharing in the author's wild imaginings.

In the lesson, students learn to identify fantasy and real-life parts of a story.

BUILDING BACKGROUND

Vocabulary Warm-up
Some words in this selection may be unfamiliar. One way to introduce students to them is to organize a **Vocabulary Quiz Show**.

shadowy   spurts   peer   cloak   greengrocer

Write each of the five words on a note card. Write the definitions for each one on another card. Then, pass the ten cards out to ten students. Have a student read one of the word cards out loud. Help with pronunciation if necessary. Ask the student with the matching definition card to read it aloud and discuss each word. Ask students to think of sentences using each word.

Prereading Strategy
Help students gain background for the selection with this **Previewing** activity. Have them read over the first four paragraphs quickly and then answer these questions:
1. What does this story seem to be about? *(a nightmare or scary story.)*
2. What characters are in the story? *(Sophie and a giant figure)*
3. Where does it take place? *(on a street in an ordinary neighborhood)*
4. What do you think will happen? *(the figure will come to Sophie's house)*
5. Ask students to explain the reasons behind their predictions. They may be based on clues found in the first three paragraphs or hunches they have.

Reading the Selection

RESPONSE STRATEGY
Students identify in the Response Notes the parts of the selection that are make-believe and those that are real life.
Sample Response:
It was four times as tall as the tallest human. (MB = make-believe); Her throat, like her whole body, was frozen with fright. (RL = real life)

CRITICAL READING SKILL
Explain to students that many skillful writers blend fantasy and real life. Some writers create a story that has a believable main character and setting, like Dahl does. Then, Dahl adds make-believe elements. Tell students that sometimes it is difficult to tell when something is fantasy or real life. To determine whether something could happen in real life, ask students to consider not only their own personal experience, but other people's as well. For example, students may say that *they* have never opened their mouths to scream and had no sound come out; however, it is possible for that to happen to someone else.

REREADING
Have students reread the selection. As they read, have them double-check the RL and MB notations they made and add any new ones they may have missed. Remind them that rather than marking each sentence, they will be marking the text in chunks of several sentences, paragraphs, or several paragraphs.

60

The second half of every *Teacher's Guide* lesson concentrates on the writing portion of the lesson. Sample responses are indicated for each activity, not to indicate right answers but rather to suggest the way students might respond. Then writing suggestions are included for helping students as they write, and a quick assessment criteria is suggested for each lesson.

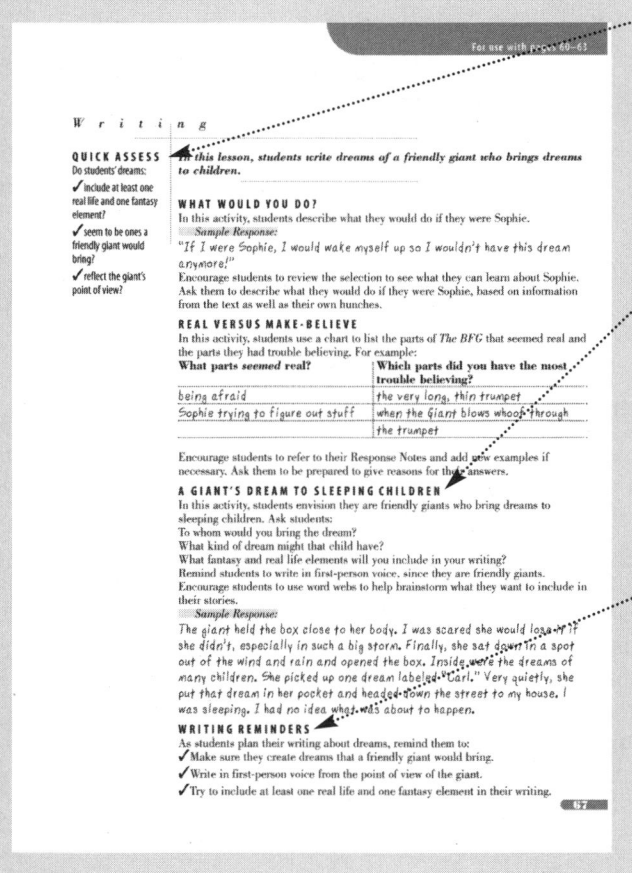

Quick Assess gives rubric for assessment.

Writing Activities are noted and explained, with sample responses indicated.

Writing Reminders provide some additional help for students as they write.

Building Better Readers

by Ruth Nathan

Introduction

Today we know enough about the teaching of reading to insure that all students become competent, life-long readers. The past half-century of research has shed light on what skilled readers know and can do as they read, and on what skilled teachers do to enhance the reading success of all their students. The *Daybooks* have kept this research in mind.

What do skilled readers know and do as they read?

Thoughtful, active, and proficient readers think about their own thinking during reading: they are "metacognitive." For example, good readers know what and when they are comprehending, and when they are not comprehending they use a variety of strategies to solve their problems. They also know how to deepen understanding by summarizing as they read, seeking clarification of unknown terms or concepts, questioning the author, using what they know to make inferences, and predicting upcoming events or concepts. Simply put, proficient readers monitor their comprehension actively. Before they read, they prepare in various ways. They might look at how texts are structured to get the "big picture," review graphics, predict what will be covered or what will happen, or bring forward relevant background knowledge. After reading, thoughtful readers reflect in a variety of ways, from discussing what they've read with friends or classmates to actively summarizing, outlining, or creating graphic organizers. Young, skilled readers tend to read widely and often. They see reading as one way into both joyful times and a successful school year.

How do skilled teachers enhance reading success for all?

Among the many features of effective instruction that successful schools use, four features stand out relative to learning to read. First, students learn strategies for doing their work. Effective teachers guide students through strategies step-by-step, giving them tips on how to read as well as how to think about their reading. Second, teachers help students make connections across instruction, curriculum, and life. They weave a web of connections within and across lessons, as well as to students' lives in and out of school. Third, students learn skills and knowledge in multiple lesson types. This means, for example, that a skill might be highlighted out of context and then reintroduced within a more natural reading experience. And, fourth, students are expected to be generative thinkers. For example, students might be asked to compare the treatment of an issue in a piece of literature with other pieces they have read or with their own life.

Building Better Readers: The *Daybook* Connection

The *Daybook* Series has brought what we know about skilled readers and skilled teaching together in one student-friendly paperback. The stories are, first and foremost, readable. The literature excerpts, all written by widely known and beloved children's authors, are varied and have been leveled in difficulty such that students are reading stories and essays at their ever-changing instructional/independent level.

With pencil in hand, students actively read by marking up the text. Children highlight and underline, draw pictures, and respond in margins as they predict, question, visualize, and think about new words during reading. By guiding students through comprehension strategies step-by-step, the *Daybook* teaches and reinforces the critical skills of finding the main idea, summarizing, making inferences, and other aspects of active and successful reading. Embedded in the *Daybooks* are strategies for monitoring comprehension, including rereading the text. Each lesson in the *Daybook* begins with activating students' prior knowledge and is followed by writing opportunities that connect the selection to other texts and students' lives. Each lesson ends with valuable writing activities, all designed to help students feel comfortable with writing as well as reading. Taken together, the approach used and strategies selected in the *Daybook* mirror current research findings. These books will encourage students to become active, engaged, and comfortable readers.

Ten Ways to Effectively Use Daybooks

by Laura Robb

"I'm such a slow reader. I don't enjoy reading."
"Reading is boring; it's just words, words, words."

These comments, spoken by middle-grade readers, reflect youngsters who are not actively involved with making meaning. The challenge we teachers face is to help every child develop that intense I-can't-put-that-book-down-feeling that motivates engaged readers to turn to books for entertainment and to learn new information. Allocating ample time each day for independent reading and ensuring that students are actively engaged in reading during that time are among teachers' most important tasks in comprehension instruction. The lessons in the *Daybooks* can transform children into active readers who connect their lives and experiences to the the finest poets and authors of fiction and nonfiction.

Research has demonstrated that the more time children read and write in authentic ways, the greater their progress in reading and writing. When children read and write at school for twenty to thirty minutes each day, they are developing their minds and imaginations in ways similar to athletes training for a sport—where daily practice is the key to progress and developing expertise. Whether a basal anthology or children's literature is the core of your literacy program, the *Daybooks* can enhance the reading and writing power of every child.

"Each of my third graders loves having their own *Daybook*—they can create a unique set of responses to the literature, and I love the extra time they spend reading, writing, and thinking." These words, spoken by a teacher required to cover a third grade anthology, illustrate the versatility of the *Daybook's* reading and writing experiences. I have identified ten ways to integrate the *Daybooks* into your reading program—ten top-notch ways that can move your students forward.

1. Introduce Students to Reading/Writing Strategies

In the *Daybook*, students practice active reading strategies such as marking a text, jotting notes while reading, predicting and questioning, and pinpointing the key details in nonfiction and fiction. Short selections are ideal for students to practice and apply the reading strategies that proficient readers use to construct meaning and link what they know to new information. The writing students complete grows out of their reading and provides opportunities to plan writing and to explore different genres, such as persuasive, informative, and descriptive paragraphs, writing dialogues, summaries, and narratives.

2. Become the Core of a Literature-based Program

As the centerpiece of your reading program, the *Daybook's* reading and writing skills (summarized in the strategy grid on pages 6–9) become the guide for your reading and writing program. All the skills and strategies that students practice are those fourth graders need to improve comprehension and recall and to develop test-taking skills. With the *Daybook* as the core of your reading program, it's easy to extend students' reading experiences for you can:

- Offer students the book from which they read a selected passage.
- Conduct an author study and have students read other books by a *Daybook* author.
- Invite students to read books and materials that relate to a theme in the *Daybook*.
- Ask students to read widely in a genre that the *Daybook* introduces.

3. Enrich Your Basal Program

I view the stories in basal anthologies as one part of a reading program. To progress, students must read widely and reflect on their reading. With the *Daybooks*, you can extend students' reading experiences and involve them in thinking and writing activities that grow out of the reading selections. Moreover, you can use selections from the *Daybook* to reteach strategies and skills, offering students the additional practice they require to deepen their understanding of pinpointing the main idea or figuring out the meaning of new words using context clues.

4. Guide New Teachers and Teachers Making the Transition to a Literature-based Program

As you read and study the *Daybook's Teacher's Guide*, you'll explore tried-and-true suggestions that model and explain how to effectively introduce each selection. During the year, as your students complete the *Daybook* lessons, they'll access research-tested reading strategies that can deepen their involvement with fiction, nonfiction, and poetry.

5. Introduce Children to Fine Authors and Literary Genres

I want all students to read literature that they will enjoy rereading and that is worth thinking about and discussing. That's why we've spent months carefully selecting pieces by such award winning authors as Roald Dahl, Judy Blume, and E. B. White, while still always being careful to maintain a cultural and gender balance. Equally as important, the authors in the *Daybooks* are favorites of children and teachers. To link reading and writing, we've invited students to experience and study a genre, then to try their hand at writing in that genre.

6. Reinforce Specific Reading/Writing Strategies

Use the *Daybook* to offer students additional practice and/or review of reading strategies and writing techniques. As students revisit and review, they deepen their understanding of how these skills and strategies work and develop the problem-solving tools that readers and writers use.

7. Works Perfectly for Small Group Instruction Led by the Teacher

The short selections in the *Daybook* are ideal for organizing small group instruction that focuses on a reading strategy, such as stating the main idea, or a writing technique, such as planning a piece. You can abandon those time-consuming searches for short, grade-level pieces; instead choose a selection and follow-up writing activity from the *Daybook*.

8. Encourage Students to Work Independently

We've designed the *Daybook*s so students can successfully complete lessons on their own or while working with a partner or small group. While students independently read and write, you're free to support students who need scaffolding.

9. Individualize Instruction

If the students in your classes are like the groups I teach, then you'll be supporting students with a wide range of reading and writing abilities. *Daybooks* simplify individualizing instruction because students can complete each lesson independently. Have grade level readers work in the fourth grade *Daybook*. Those reading above grade level can complete the *Daybooks* for grades five or six. By individualizing instruction, you enable every child to start at his or her independent reading level and slowly move forward.

10. Save Teachers Time

The hours you set aside to rummage through stacks of books and magazines searching for literature for your students can now be used for responding to students' written work. When you include the *Daybooks* in your curriculum, you have a collection of the finest literature as well as reading, writing, and vocabulary skills and strategies that relate to each selection—and it's all there in one ready-to-use book!

Assessment of Writing — Some Guidelines

by Vicki Spandel

As a reading and writing teacher, you may be thinking that not all student writing within the *Daybooks* lends itself to assessment. Because the *Daybooks* are interactive, they invite students to participate as active readers, underlining, highlighting, posing questions, and making notes in the margins. Such writings would not normally be assessed, except in the sense that you may wish to check that students are indeed participating actively by making notes and responding to the text as they go. This is important for at least two reasons. First, we believe that this interaction makes students more engaged and therefore more attentive readers. In addition, these "small" writing activities provide practice in skills required for a culminating larger writing activity that rounds out each lesson. These larger pieces of writing do lend themselves to assessment, and here we offer you some guidelines on four important characteristics you might look for in your students' work.

1. Understanding of Key Concepts

Each lesson has a focus, a point to make, or a skill to teach. Some of the key concepts around which lessons are built include identification of a main idea, use of detail to create pictures in a reader's mind, learning to grasp the meaning of a word from the way it is used in context, or discovering clues in a text to help unravel a character's personality. Since the lessons interweave reading and writing, students first have an opportunity to see how each concept or skill looks in the hands of a professional writer. This is where students' notetaking and underlining or highlighting become so important. What they notice in the writing of others, they can eventually incorporate into their own writing. This is the first thing you want to look for.

For example, one lesson provides practice on main idea and supporting details. Students read about a subject such as laughter and make notes, then use a main idea planner to write a paragraph of their own. As you look at your students' original writing, you should look for a reflection of the lesson learned: using details to make a main idea clear. Is there a main idea? Is it easy for you to identify? Do the details relate? Do they help make the main idea clear? If these things are true, then you can say safely that the student has internalized the point of the lesson. As a second example, you might look at a lesson on personification. Students first read and respond to an example of personification. Then, students are asked to adopt the voice of an animal and write from this unique perspective. Those who have internalized the concept of personification will show this in their writing through an identifiable, accurate voice that comes from this new perspective. Through the writing, each student will "become" the animal character he or she is portraying.

2. Thoughtfulness

Both reading and writing are thoughtful, reflective activities. In students' writing, you want to see evidence of this reflection and thoughtfulness—a characteristic some teachers might call "depth." It is quite possible for students to breeze through a lesson without really asking, "Which words create meaning? Which passages are memorable enough to underline? Which phrases give me important clues about the point this author is trying to make?" Students who read this way, however, will have difficulty projecting much thoughtfulness in their own writing—simply because they have not taken time to notice what skilled writers do to create meaning.

For example, in another lesson students read and consider a folktale and are asked to identify the story's meaning. A surface sort of response might be "to tell a story about two animals." While this is true on a literal level, it does not reveal much probing into the real reasons authors write, and more specifically, the reasons authors tell folktales. More thoughtful responses might be—"to make readers think," "to teach readers about life," "to show what people are like," "to make us laugh at ourselves," or "to teach lessons." Reflective responses are often striking, surprising, and even provocative. They may raise questions in your own mind—or push you to a new level of thought. They may make you see a piece of literature in a way you had not anticipated. Look for writing that shows insight, in-depth understanding, a willingness to question, or an unusual point of view; any of these will tell you, "This was a student who put real thought into his or her writing." Appreciate the student who does not settle for an obvious answer, but who tosses a question around in his or her head for a time and insists on responding in an original way.

3. Attention to Detail

Young reader-writers reflect attention to detail in a number of ways. One is through the ability to make connections to their own lives and experiences. Writers such as Roald Dahl are famous for their perception and sensitivity to the details around them. When we share their literature, we invite students to share in this perception, too—to tune into their own world (using Dahl or another author as a model) and note the details they might otherwise have missed. In "Reading Authors," students have several opportunities to make connections between the readings and the events or images from their own experience. The power of these connections depends largely on attention to detail.

For instance, in a lesson "Thinking About Characters," students read about a fourth grader named Peter Hatcher. Readers who are inexperienced in looking for detail may simply see Peter as a young boy with a new pet. They may not notice the details of Peter's apartment building, the way Peter feels about his family, or Peter's excitement about his new pet. Perceptive readers will pick up these little details and clues. When they fill out a character profile, it will do more than describe Peter's actions and will touch on his motivations and feelings. Detailed writing is thorough and satisfying; it digs beneath the obvious. It holds your attention. It paints a picture in your mind, and often evokes feelings as well. These are the things you should look for in your students' writing.

In addition, writers who read for detail find it easy to summarize what they have learned. In a lesson "Is It Important?," readers are asked to read not just for pleasure but also to gain information. Those students with a strong sense of detail will look for the unusual or intriguing as they read, and then create writing that is both accurate and attention-getting. First, they will capture details correctly. But in addition, like all good nonfiction writers, they will grab and hold your interest by using details you can't ignore. In students' nonfiction writing, look for accuracy and detail that counts.

4. Growth as Readers and Writers

As students record their thoughts and reactions in the *Daybook,* they create a kind of portfolio. Like all portfolios kept over time, this one will show growth—one of the most important qualities you can look for in your students' work. What does growth look like? How will you recognize it?

First, you may simply see an expanding fluency, a willingness to write more text and to include more detail, more opinion, more personal observation. In addition, you may sense that your young writers are writing with more ease, that writing is becoming a natural and comfortable thing to do. You are likely to see more marginal notes, more sensitive and thoughtful questions, more text everywhere—and less hesitancy to share personal thoughts and feelings, even when others may not agree.

Second, you may find that your students are more creative, adventurous, and experimental in their writing. Their sense of voice may grow stronger, so that the text takes on the power that comes from expressiveness, individuality, and confidence. You may not work your way through these lessons exactly in the order they're presented, of course, but let's say you did. You might then make some comparisons by looking at early writing, then later pieces, to see how voice and confidence have grown. An early lesson in *Daybook* 4 presents students with the story "Hare, Otter, Monkey, and Badger" by Josepha Sherman. Students are then asked to come up with an ending of their own, based on predictions they've made. Their responses may be very lively and filled with voice—or they may be slightly more restrained and tentative. After all, this may be one of their first attempts at this kind of writing. How much will this early voice grow? You can tell by comparing this writing with later pieces. It is likely that you will hear an emerging personal voice that reveals both a strong sense of self and an awareness of an audience. Strong writers never forget that they are writing to someone; in fact, every sample in this *Daybook* was chosen because it revealed that audience awareness. When you see and hear awareness of audience in your students' writing, you know the voice is strong.

Third, expect growth in the amount and quality of detail you see within their text. In one lesson, readers focus on sensory detail, first noticing the detail-rich text, then creating a sensory passage of their own, bringing an animal to life through sights, sounds, smells, and feelings. Compare the detail of this text with that of earlier writings. Is it more vivid? Are the words more precise? Is the picture more clear in your mind than those created much earlier? If so, then the writer has grown both as an observer and as a recorder of detail.

You may also see growth in such things as vocabulary (a willingness to stretch and use new words and an ability to use new words accurately), sentence fluency (longer sentences, more variety, a more natural flow), and control of conventions (spelling, punctuation, grammar, capitalization). No one thing should be the focus of your measure of growth; but together these many qualities of writing give a full picture of how a student is gaining in confidence and control.

Once students have worked with the *Daybook* for a time, you can look inside and see, through their comments and their writings, that they have traveled on a journey of understanding as readers and writers. The final, most significant assessment is this: Have they taken the best of what they have observed in the writing of others and woven it into their own text? This noticing, borrowing, and interweaving is what the *Daybook* journey is all about.

The *Daybook* attempts to build better readers—ones that read actively, marking up the text, highlighting, questioning, predicting, and visualizing. The numerous, brief selections give students many opportunities to become more fluent, more active readers.

But the many different selections also pose challenges for younger readers. With each selection, students meet new vocabulary, new subjects, new characters—in short, new challenges. To help with difficult selections, the Reading Workshop presented here attempts to give you some tools to use with students during the reading process. At each step in the process—before they read, during their reading, and after their reading—you can help them succeed. This Reading Workshop can serve as a handy toolkit of strategies to use as needed.

This workshop has 3 parts:

- **Before Reading**

- **During Reading**

- **After Reading**

Within each part, reading strategies are explained and then followed by a do-it-yourself blackline master for you to adapt to individual *Daybook* lessons.

Before Reading

Before students open their *Daybooks*, your **goals** for helping students before they read are:

1. **to introduce key vocabulary**

2. **to build readiness and anticipation**

3. **to set the purpose for reading**

Among the better **strategies** for accomplishing these goals are:

➤ **Word or concept webs**

➤ **Vocabulary inventory**

➤ **Anticipation guides**

➤ **Think-pair-and-share**

Word or Concept Web

What Is It?

A word or concept web can build a common background before students read. By writing the key word or concept in the center of a web and then brainstorming with the class or in small groups, all students can pool their common knowledge of a subject. Webs often work best in building background for animals, things, or concepts.

How to Introduce It

Either in small groups of 4-6 or as a whole class, hand out copies of the web diagram. Have students write the name of the animal, thing, or concept in the middle circle. Then brainstorm with students to answer some key questions about it.

- What does it look like?
- Where does it live or where do you see it?
- What are some examples of it?
- When do you see it?
- What do you think about it?
- How does it feel?

What It Looks Like

A word or concept web looks something like this once it is completed.

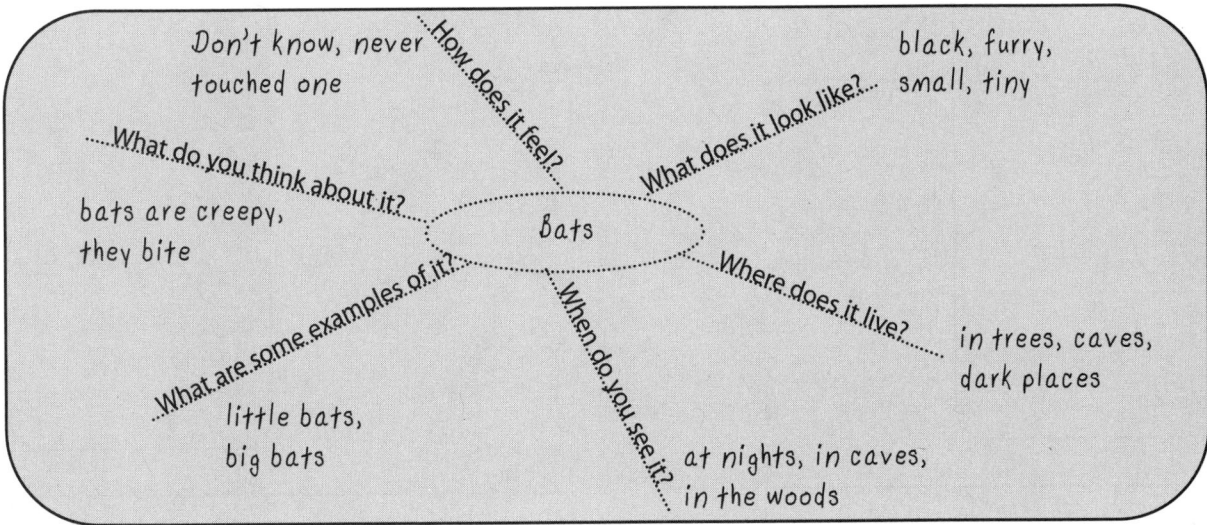

What to Look Out For

Remember that the goal of introducing a subject or idea in a word web is to build background. The exercise should be brief, involving a number of students, but not strive to be comprehensive. What matters is that students have a frame of reference as they begin reading and their minds are activated.

WORD WEB

Selection:

Author:

Write the name of the place, animal, or idea in the center circle. Then answer the questions around it.

What does it look like?

What are some examples of it?

...How does it feel?

When do you see it?

Where does it live?

What do you think about it?

Vocabulary Inventory

What Is It?

A vocabulary inventory gives you an understanding of how familiar students are with the vocabulary of a selection. Quick and easy, the inventory can be a great way to begin a lesson with challenging words, as well as a way to start students thinking about the selection, because the words can suggest the subject and be the starting point for making predictions. You make one by choosing ten words that are important to the selection.

How to Introduce It

Explain to students that you want to find out how familiar they are with some of the words in the selection. Be sure to say that this is not a test. Students will not be graded on the results. The purpose is to start students thinking about some of the words from the selection and what the selection may be about.

What It Looks Like

A vocabulary inventory looks something like this:

VOCABULARY INVENTORY

The Kid's Guide to Money

By Steve Otfinoski

Pages 58-60

Look carefully at each word below. Then mark whether you know the word (+), whether it seems familiar (?), or whether you don't know the word at all (0).

+ I Know This Word

? Seems Familiar

0 Don't Know This Word

1. _____ loans   6. _____ bank
2. _____ deposit   7. _____ guardian
3. _____ interest   8. _____ savings
4. _____ customers   9. _____ money
5. _____ autimated   10. _____ teller machine

Now make a prediction. What do you think this selection will be about?

_____

_____

What to Look Out For

A vocabulary inventory will give you an idea if students can handle the vocabulary in the selection. If students are not familiar with more than half of the words, chances are the selection will pose strong reading challenges for them. Begin the lesson by using the **Vocabulary Warm-up** in the *Teacher's Guide*. If students are familiar with most of the words, preteaching vocabulary probably is not necessary.

VOCABULARY INVENTORY

Selection: ....

Author: ....

Look carefully at each word below. Then mark whether you know the word (+), whether it seems familiar (?), or whether you don't know the word at all (0).

+   Know This Word

?   Seems Familiar

0   Don't Know This Word

1. _____ ....   6. _____ ....

2. _____ ....   7. _____ ....

3. _____ ....   8. _____ ....

4. _____ ....   9. _____ ....

5. _____ ....   10. _____ ....

Now make a prediction. What do you think this selection will be about?

....

....

....

Anticipation Guide

What Is It?

An anticipation guide serves two purposes: it helps motivate students to want to read a selection and it builds some background about the selection before students begin reading. As a result, it becomes a powerful tool in your arsenal for creating reading readiness in your students. To make an anticipation guide, write 3–5 statements about the subject of the story or article.

How to Introduce It

Ask students to form small groups of 4-6 or work through the activity as a whole class. Tell students that, before they read, you want to find out what they already know about the subject of this next selection. Then hand out copies of the anticipation guide that you create from the blackline master on the next page.

Have students write whether they agree or disagree with each statement. Then, after recording their answers, ask students to share them with their classmates. Tell students that there are no right or wrong answers, but encourage them to discuss with each other places where their answers are different from others in the group.

What It Looks Like

An anticipation guide looks something like this once it is prepared.

Read each statement. Circle whether you agree or disagree. Then discuss your answers with a partner.

Agree	**Disagree**	1. Goldfish are always orange.
Agree	**Disagree**	2. Goldfish don't live more than a few days in an aquarium.
Agree	**Disagree**	3. A goldfish can be a good pet.

What to Look Out For

The idea behind an anticipation guide is to build background for students and motivation for what they are about to read. Encourage students to form questions, not argue about who is right and who is wrong. Have students share information they know and end by making predictions about what they think will happen. Then, after they are finished reading, have students come back to see if they still hold the same opinions that they did at the beginning.

ANTICIPATION GUIDE

Selection: ....

Author: ....

Circle whether you agree or disagree with each statement. Compare your answers with a partner. Talk about what you agreed and disagreed about. Then, write a prediction of what you think this selection will be about.

<u>**Before Reading**</u>   <u>**After Reading**</u>

Agree   Disagree   1. .... **Agree   Disagree**

....

....

Agree   Disagree   2. .... **Agree   Disagree**

....

....

Agree   Disagree   3. .... **Agree   Disagree**

....

....

Agree   Disagree   4. .... **Agree   Disagree**

....

....

Agree   Disagree   5. .... **Agree   Disagree**

....

....

What do you think this selection will be about?

....

....

....

Then, after you are finished reading, come back and answer each statement again. Did any of your answers change? Why?

T h i n k - P a i r - a n d - S h a r e

What Is It?

A Think-Pair-and-Share activity introduces a selection in a fun, interactive way, gently leading reluctant readers into the act of reading. It gives students some background about a selection and piques interest in what will happen.

How to Introduce It

If time permits, ask students to form small groups of 4-6. If possible, put each sentence on a separate strip of paper. Give each student in the group one sentence, and ask him or her to read it aloud to the others. Tell students that their job is to decide in what order the sentences appear in the selection and what the selection is about.

What It Looks Like

Here is an example of a Think-Pair-and-Share activity.

Think-Pair-and-Share

Read each quote below from the story. Put the sentences in the order in which you think they appear in the selection.

_____ 1. "It gave her great pleasure to watch him eating worms."

_____ 2. "The next day, to pay Mr. Twit back for the frog trick, Mrs. Twit sneaked out into the garden and dug up some worms."

_____ 3. "Hey, my spaghetti's moving!' cried Mr. Twit, poking around in it with his fork."

What do you think this story is about?

_____

_____

_____

What to Look Out For

Having students work in groups for Think-Pair-and-Share activities can become noisy, because students are reading the sentences from the story and discussing them. Try to keep students focused. The idea is to help students construct some idea of what the story might be about and to generate interest in reading the story.

THINK-PAIR-AND-SHARE

Selection: ....

Author: ....

Read each sentence to the others in your group. Then put the sentences in the order in which you think they appear in the selection.

✂ -

1.

✂ -

2.

✂ -

3.

✂ -

4.

✂ -

5.

✂ -

What do you think this story is about?

....

....

During Reading

While students are reading in their *Daybook*, the primary **goals** are:

1. **to build active reading and involvement**

2. **to increase comprehension**

Among the best **strategies** for accomplishing these goals are:

➢ **Double-entry journals**

➢ **Retelling**

➢ **Using graphic organizers**

  • **story star**

  • **timeline**

  • **storyboard**

  • **main idea and details**

  • **Venn diagram**

  • **plot chart**

Across the country, teachers have numerous ways of improving comprehension. Students need not know ALL of the strategies available. Strive instead to introduce a few KEY strategies that students can use again and again. Students need to know a few good comprehension strategies, but also know how and when to use them.

Try to introduce your students to these comprehension strategies over the year.

Double-Entry Journal

What Is It?

A Double-Entry Journal is a way to help students look closely at passages in the text. Often called a response journal, a quote or sentence from a selection is written in the lefthand column, and then students respond to it by writing their reactions in the righthand column. It builds students' ability to comprehend and interpret text.

How to Introduce It

Tell students that you will show them a way to get more from what they are reading. Write a quote from a text on the board and ask students to do the same in a notebook. Then write your thoughts or response to the quote, and ask students to do the same. Then discuss your response and explain why you wrote that with the class. Ask student volunteers to share their responses.

What It Looks Like

Here is an example of what a Double-Entry Journal looks like.

Quote	My thoughts and conclusions
"Jesse chewed his palm as he moved up the line."	
"He looked at the kids still in line, then at Michael who yelled, 'You can do it!'"	
"When the next number was called, Michael jogged off the field with his head held high."	
"'Don't be scared,'" Michael said with his mouth full of ham sandwich, though he knew Jesse's batting was no good."	
"Jesse said he thought he did and imitated Michael's swing until Michael said, 'Yeah, you got it.'"	

What to Look Out For

Double-Entry Journals can be used at almost any grade and are especially helpful in getting students to look closely at poetry. But students often have a difficult time choosing good passages from the selection on their own and may need guidance in which passages to select. The goal is for them to select meaningful passages that lend themselves to interpretation.

DOUBLE-ENTRY JOURNAL

Selection:

Author:

Write a quote from the story in the lefthand column below. In the column next to it, write your thoughts and feelings about the quote. Then write two or more quotes in the story and your response to them.

Quote	My Thoughts and Feelings
1.	
2.	
3.	
4.	

Retelling

What Is It?

A retelling is a "telling again" in the student's own words. Just as in conversation when, to show you understand, you might say, "What I hear you saying is . . .," retelling gives students a chance to put the message in their own words. The act of processing what they comprehend and translating it into words of their own helps students understand—and remember.

How to Introduce It

Tell students that you want to help them put what they read into their own words. Explain that, by retelling what they have read, they will comprehend more of what they are reading.

What It Looks Like

Often retelling is simply done orally. You ask, "What did you learn?" or "What has happened so far?" In written form, a retelling can take a number of different forms.

EXAMPLE 1

EXAMPLE 2

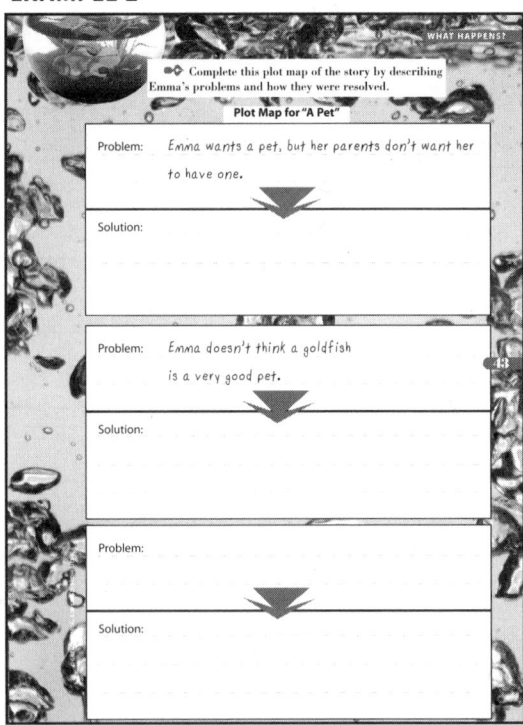

What to Look Out For

Students may not give perfect summaries in their initial retellings. Look instead for evidence that they are processing the information and putting it in their own words. By reading over what they have retold, students will themselves find ways their retellings can be improved. More than the final product, what's important is the greater comprehension the activity of retelling yields.

RETELLING

Selection:

Author:

Write down one idea from each paragraph or the 4 big ideas you remember. Put the ideas in the order in which they occurred.

1.

2.

3.

4.

RETELLING

Selection:

Author:

Write down one idea from each paragraph or the 4-5 ideas you remember. Then write what you think is the main idea or biggest idea overall.

Paragraph 1 Idea:

Paragraph 2 Idea:

Paragraph 3 Idea:

Paragraph 4 Idea:

Paragraph 5 Idea:

Main Idea:

Graphic Organizers

What Is It?

A graphic organizer is a way to help students visualize information they are reading. Sequence, cause and effect, plot, characters, timelines—in short, almost all of the abstract ideas that come from reading—can be organized and visualized better by learning how to use graphic organizers.

How to Introduce It

Explain that an organizer can help students collect and sort through all of the information they are receiving as they read. Explain too that different organizers can be helpful for different kinds of writing. For stories or fiction, the organizers called character maps, plot charts, and storyboards generally work best. For nonfiction, suggest that students use timelines, webs, cause-effect, and Venn diagrams.

What It Looks Like

Here is an example of one kind of graphic organizer.

Character Map

What he says:	How others feel about him:

Bobby

How he feels:	What I think about him:

What to Look Out For

Students will need to become familiar with a number of different graphic organizers and be shown which ones work best with which kinds of writing. Using the organizer tends to be the easy part. The difficulty for students is to know which type of organizer to use. You can help students learn which graphic organizer to use by introducing a limited number initially and then discussing which one might work best in different situations.

Name:

Graphic Organizer
STORY STAR

Selection:

Author:

Write down the answer to each question after reading the story.

Who?

What happened?

Where?

Story Title

When?

How did it turn out?

Graphic Organizer
TIMELINE

Selection:

Author:

Write the event that happens first in the column Time/Date on the left.
Beside it, write what happened. Write down each major event or occurrence.

Time/Date	Events

Graphic Organizer
STORYBOARD

Selection:

Author:

Sketch four memorable scenes or events from the story. Next to each sketch, write a brief description of what happens.

1.

2.

3.

4.

Graphic Organizer
MAIN IDEA AND DETAILS

Selection:

Author:

Write down one detail from each paragraph or the 4-5 details you can remember about the subject. Then write what you think is the overall main idea of the selection.

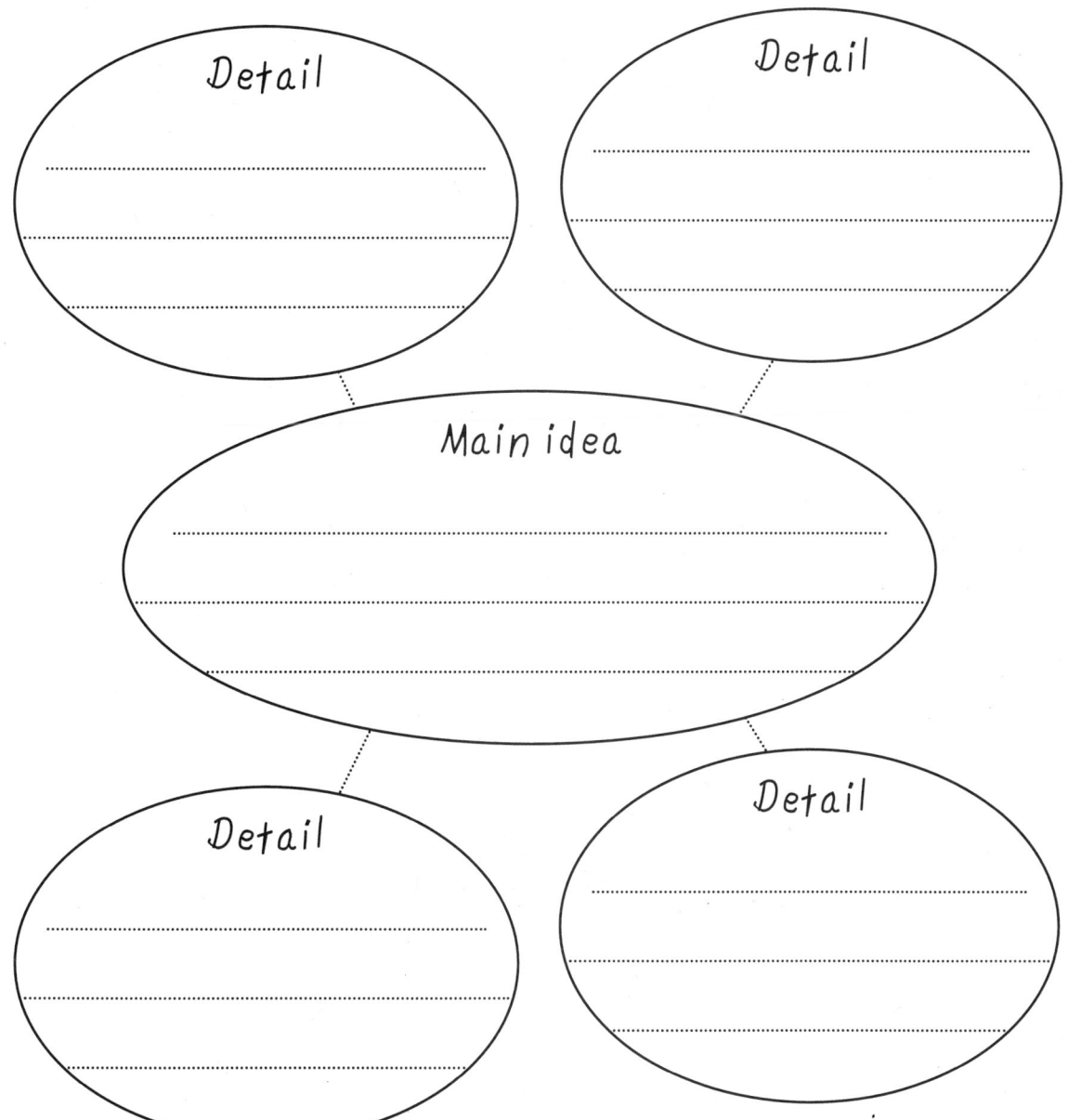

Graphic Organizer
VENN DIAGRAM

Selection:

Author:

Use this Venn diagram to show how two characters or things are alike and different. Write the name of one thing you are comparing on each line. Write what is special or different about each thing in the outside part of the circles (#1 and #2). In the center, write how the two things or characters are similar (#3).

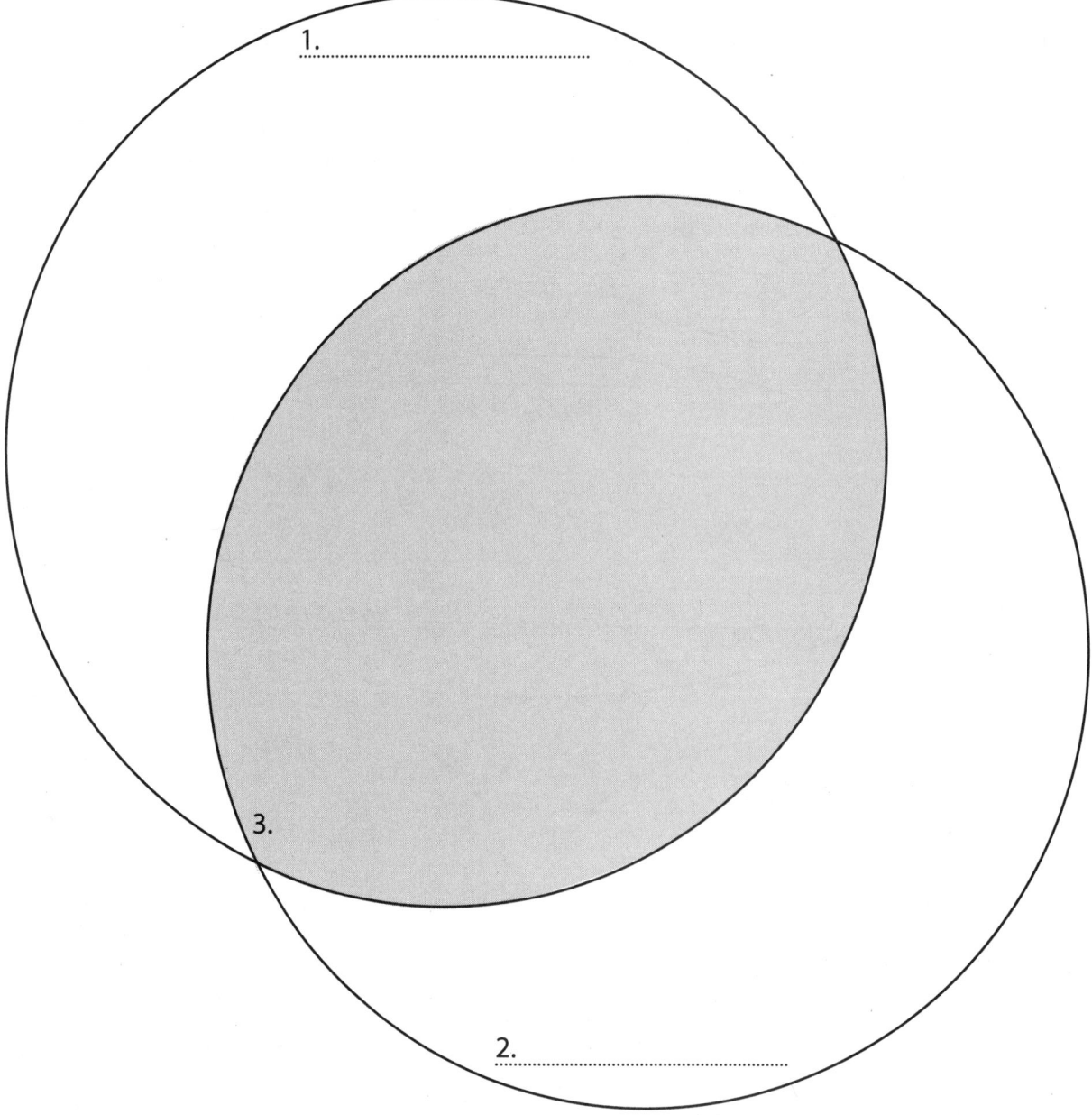

1.

3.

2.

Name:

Graphic Organizer
PLOT CHART

Selection:

Author:

Use this plot chart to show the major events in the story. Begin with the first event in the story. Write it at the bottom beside Event 1. Then list the other events leading up to the climax, when the problem of the story is resolved.

Write the problem and its solution in the boxes at the bottom of the page.

Peak Event:

Event 4

Event 3

Event 2

Event 1

Problem	Solution

©Great Source. Permission is granted to copy this page.

After Reading

After students are finished reading in their *Daybook*s, the primary **goals** are:

1. **to reread to increase comprehension even more**

2. **to make the reading their own**

3. **to remember or retain what is read**

Among the best **strategies** for accomplishing these goals are:

➤ **Rereading with a purpose**
  • **asking questions**
  • **predictions**

➤ **Summarizing**
  • **story string**
  • **main idea and details**

➤ **Organizing what you learned**
  • **character maps**
  • **story cards**
  • **plot charts**
  • **charts (for nonfiction)**
  • **cause-effect charts (for nonfiction)**

Readers comprehend at different rates, and they comprehend different things from a selection. By rereading with a purpose, any reader can go back and find the information (about a character, story, subject) that they need.

Creating a summary or graphic organizer is another way for a reader to collect what he or she has learned. It is also a product, a way for a reader to work through and process the information, which is vital for retention and recalling the information later.

Encourage your students to reread, but with a purpose. Good readers go back into a text all of the time to gather more information or confirm a detail that they only partially remember. After reading a selection, help students get in the habit of rereading by using the strategies above for collecting and retaining what they read.

Rereading with a Purpose

What Is It?

By asking questions before reading or making predictions while reading, students set a purpose for their reading. This gives a reason for the activity of reading. They want to find out something. Too often students read without any purpose. When asked, they respond that they are reading a selection because they were told to read it. Students need to learn how to set a purpose for themselves before they read. The purpose helps make them more active readers and will help them get more from what they read.

How to Introduce It

Help students set a simple purpose before they read any selection. In the *Daybooks*, the response strategy (or active reading strategy) sets the purpose for reading. Students are told what they should mark, underline, highlight, or circle—in other words, what to look for.

Point out the response strategies in the lessons to students. Tell them that the strategies signal what they should look for in the selection as they read.

Then, after an initial reading, ask students to double back and look for the details or specific information noted in the response strategy. Most of the time marking the text and reading with comprehension will tax the ability of most students. Encourage students to mark other details as they reread.

What It Looks Like

Here is an example of one kind of activity that requires students to go back into the text and reread to find details about causes and effects.

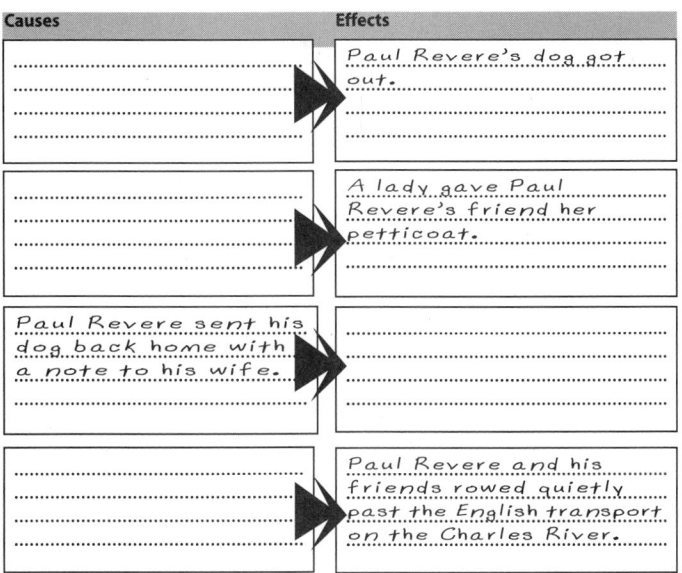

Causes	Effects
	Paul Revere's dog got out.
	A lady gave Paul Revere's friend her petticoat.
Paul Revere sent his dog back home with a note to his wife.	
	Paul Revere and his friends rowed quietly past the English transport on the Charles River.

What to Look Out For

Students will find rereading hard work. Encourage students as they reread, pointing out to them that expert readers are expert *rereaders.* Many students will think that they "didn't get it," when in fact rereading is normal—and necessary.

Rereading with a Purpose:
ASKING QUESTIONS

Selection:

Author:

Before and as you read, write down questions that you want to know more about.
Then, reread the selection to find answers to your questions. Write your answers in
the middle column. In the last column, write the evidence from the selection that
explains how you know.

Question	My Answer	How Do I Know?

Rereading with a Purpose:
PREDICTIONS

Selection:

Author:

While you are reading, stop a few times and write down your predictions. Note the page in the first column and your prediction in the middle column. Then, reread the selection once you have finished and, in the last column, note what really happened.

page number	I predicted . . .	What really happened . . .

Summarizing

What Is It?

A summary is a retelling of the important parts of a selection. For nonfiction, a summary tells the main idea and important details about it. For fiction, a summary recounts the major events in the story line.

How to Introduce It

Help students see what a summary is by using graphic organizers. Tell students that they will need to use an organizer like a Story String for stories or fiction. It helps them record events in the order they happen—that is, chronological order. Tell students they will need to use a Main Idea and Detail organizer for nonfiction selections. It helps them note specific details about a subject and decide what is the larger, main idea about the subject.

What It Looks Like

Here is an example of one kind of activity that requires students to go back into the text and reread to find details about causes and effects.

Subject			
Detail #1	Detail #2	Detail #3	Detail #4
Main Idea			

What to Look Out For

Students find it difficult to distinguish the main idea from the supporting details. Be sure to model sorting out the main idea from the smaller details for students at least once. Students will also need help matching the appropriate organizer to the kind of text they are reading, so you may need to choose the appropriate organizer for them the first few times.

Summarizing:
STORY STRING

Selection:

Author:

After reading, go back through the story one more time. Write down the key events that occur. Put them in the order in which they happen.

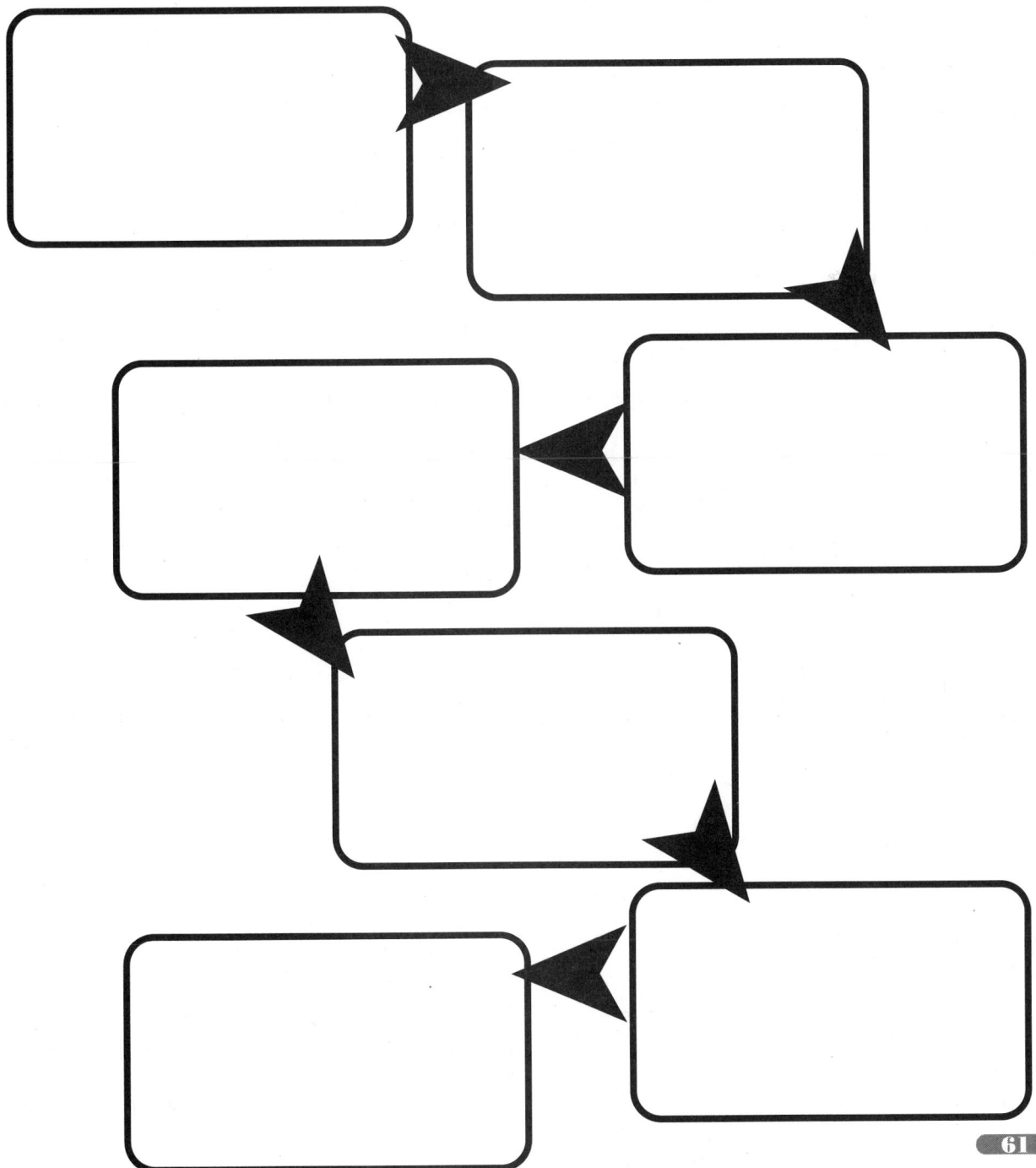

Summarizing:
MAIN IDEA AND DETAILS

Selection: _____

Author: _____

After you finish reading, look back over the selection and the highlighting you made. First list four supporting details you learned about the subject. Then, decide what the author says about the subject. Write that as the main idea.

Summary

Main Idea: _____

_____

Supporting Details:

1. _____

2. _____

3. _____

4. _____

Organizing What You Learned

What Is It?

Organizing what you learned simply means taking time after reading to collect and organize the information. Quite often students stop reading with the last word in a selection. Helping students collect and organize what they have learned will show them a way to get the most out of the time they invest in reading.

How to Introduce It

Help students understand that reading is a process, not an act. Explain that, once students reach the end of a selection, they have more to do. Now they need to collect what they have learned. By taking notes, filling out a cause-and-effect chart, or creating a web diagram, they can get more from what they read and remember it better.

What It Looks Like

Here is one chart from *Daybook* 4 that collects what students learned about elephants:

Question	Your Answer	How Do You Know?
How does Peter act?		
How does Peter feel about others?		
How does Peter feel about himself?		

What to Look Out For

Students will probably not see why they have to do even more work after they finish reading. Help them see that, by collecting what they learned, they will remember more of what they read.

Organizing Fiction:
CHARACTER MAP

Selection:

Author:

After you finish reading fiction, take a minute to go back over the selection. Use the character map below to organize what you have learned about the main character. First, write the character's name in the center. Then fill in each box.

What the character says:	What others say about the character:
How the character looks:	How I feel about the character:

Character:

Organizing Fiction:
STORYCARDS

Selection: _____

Author: _____

After you finish reading a story, spend some time to go back over the selection. Use the storycards below to organize what happened. Fill in information about the title, author, characters, setting, and plot.

Storycard

Author

Title

Characters

Setting

Plot

Organizing Fiction:
PLOT CHART

Selection: _____

Author: _____

After you finish reading, an easy way to keep track of what happened is to describe what happened in the beginning, middle, and end of a story. Use the plot chart below to organize what happened. Write 2 things that happen at the beginning, 2 things that happen in the middle of the story, and 2 things that happen at the end.

Plot Chart

#1	#2

#3	#4

#5	#6

Organizing Nonfiction:
CHARTS

Selection:

Author:

Write the names of specific things you learned about (countries, animals, types of things) in the column on the left. Across the top, write the names of general categories (for example, what animals eat, where they live, and so on). Then reread the selection, filling in the chart.

Specific details	General categories			

Organizing Nonfiction:
CAUSE AND EFFECT

Selection:

Author:

Reread the selection and use the chart below to help you organize the causes and effects. Write the causes you find in the lefthand boxes. In the righthand boxes, write the effects that result from those causes.

Causes and Effects

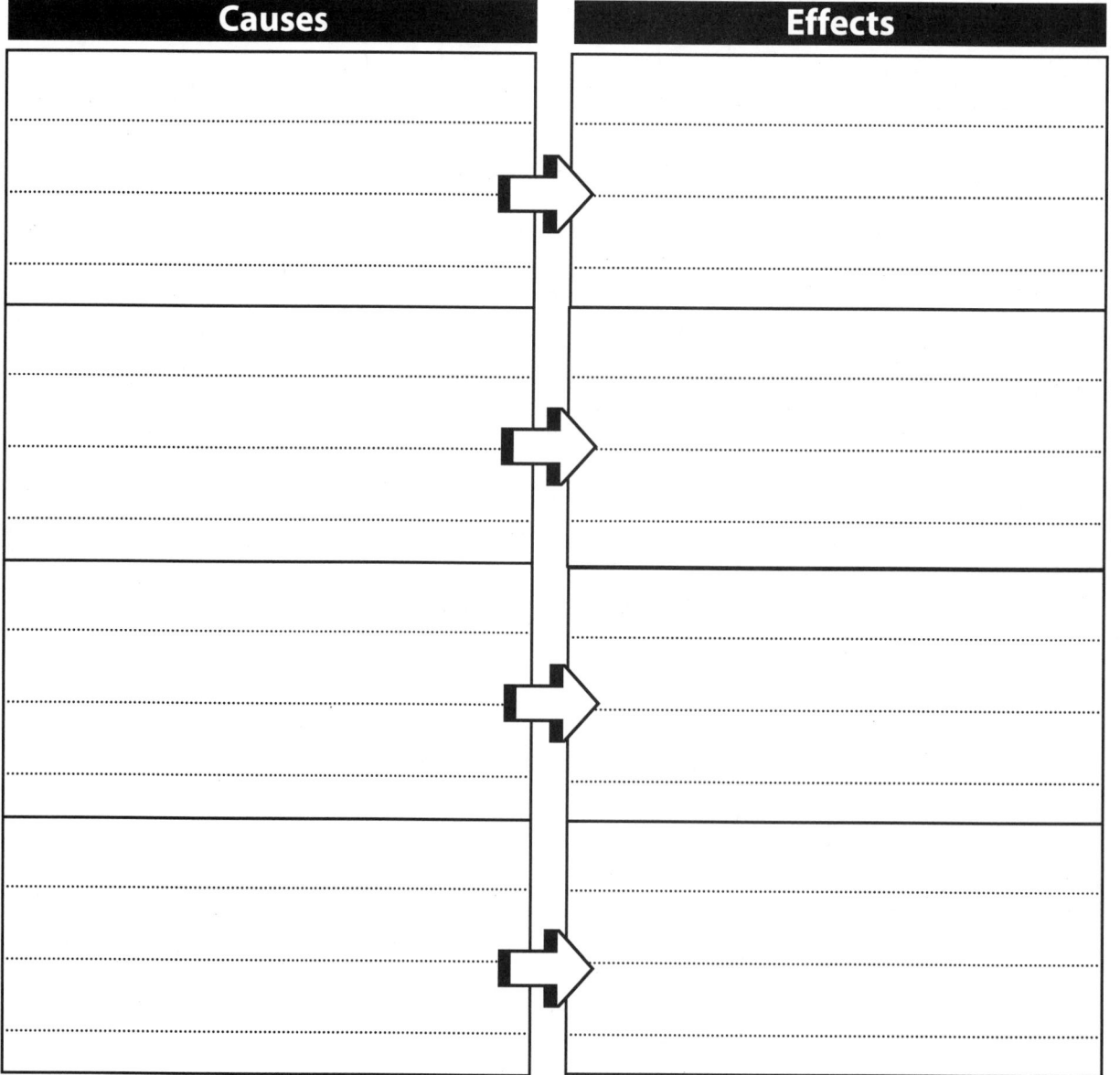

Causes	Effects

LESSON RESOURCES

Unit Overview

In this unit, students learn the skills of active reading by practicing how to mark up a text, underline, highlight, predict, question, and visualize. The purpose of these initial lessons is to start students marking in the *Daybook* and writing in the Response Notes. The active reading skills introduced in these first lessons will be practiced throughout the *Daybook,* so students do not need mastery of active reading before progressing. Rather, the idea of the introductory unit is to start them on the way toward becoming active readers.

Reading the Art

Give students a moment to look at the opener. Then, in small groups of 3 or 4, have students discuss these questions:

- What do they see in the artwork?
- What things does the girl appear to be holding?
- Why are these things important?
- Why is this art a good choice to introduce a unit on *Active Reading?*

Literature Focus

Lesson	Literature
1. Mark Up the Text	**Jane Yolen,** from "The Lad" This fiction selection is about a young man's attempts to prove himself by staring down others.
2. Visualize	**Jane Yolen,** from "The Lad" In this second part of the story, the lad stares down his parents and leaves his home to stare down the world.
3. Predict	**Jane Yolen,** from "The Lad" In the next part of the story, the lad continues to stare down a watchman and then two soldiers.
4. Question	**Jane Yolen,** from "The Lad" In this fourth part of the story, the lad slips past the soldiers and into the castle, where he meets the king.
5. Apply the Strategies	**Jane Yolen,** from "The Lad" In the conclusion, the lad attempts to stare down the king, but an old man challenges him to stare down the sun, and the lad tries to do it.

Reading Focus

Lesson	Reading Skill
1. Mark Up the Text	Mark, underline, and highlight parts of a text.
2. Visualize	Create images in your mind as you read and sketch them.
3. Predict	Use what you know and clues from a story to figure out what will happen next.
4. Question	Ask questions about parts of the story that you don't understand, such as unfamiliar words or a character's actions.
5. Apply the Strategies	Use active reading strategies of marking, visualizing, predicting, and questioning.

Mark Up the Text

Before Reading

FOCUS

As you read, ask yourself: What do I think will happen next?

In this introductory mini-lesson, students learn a skill of active readers—to mark passages in the text in order to find important information.

BUILDING BACKGROUND

Explain to students that marking up the text is a skill good readers use to get the most out of their reading. Highlighting interesting words and passages and "talking back" to the text by writing their own comments and questions helps students concentrate on the reading. In this way, they gain a deeper knowledge of the text, which in turn aids their retention and understanding.

Reading the Introduction

Read through the first paragraph with students. Explain that as active readers of this *Daybook*, they will be asked to mark up the book. Remind students that they cannot mark up the other textbooks that belong to the school.

Reading the Selection

Read "The Lad" by Jane Yolen, stopping at the bottom of the page. Ask students:
➤ What types of sample responses do you see on the page?
➤ Why do you think "...stare down his mother and father" is underlined and starred?
➤ What sentence is underlined, and why?
➤ What types of written responses do you see in the Response Notes?
➤ What new comment could you add?

Point out to students that they will be asked to write different types of comments in the Response Notes throughout this book. The passages they highlight in the text, along with their Response Notes, will help them complete activities related to the reading. Remind students that they can review this page at any time as a model for the types of responses they might have to the reading.

Visualize

Before Reading

In this introductory mini-lesson, students learn to visualize a piece of writing as they read.

BUILDING BACKGROUND

Explain to students that to visualize something from a story takes concentration. This focus aids understanding and retention by itself, but when students sketch what they visualize, they will have an even clearer memory of the character or event. Sometimes they will be asked to sketch something in the Response Notes. Other times it will be an activity as part of the lesson.

Reading the Introduction

Have students read the introductory paragraph. Ask them why it is important to "see" a selection as they read.

Reading the Selection

Read the next part of "The Lad" by Jane Yolen, stopping at the bottom of the page. Ask students:

➤ What part did the student in the sample choose to sketch?

➤ Why do you think he or she chose that part?

➤ How do you think sketching parts of a story could help you become a better reader?

➤ What new part in this segment would you choose to highlight and illustrate? Draw your own sketch in the Response Notes.

Remind students that they can review this page at any time to review how to use the Response Notes to sketch what they see.

Predict

Before Reading

In this introductory mini-lesson, students learn to predict what will happen.

BUILDING BACKGROUND
Explain to students that a prediction may relate to a character's actions in the future or to the progression of the story as a whole. Sometimes students will underline text that relates to a prediction. Other times, students will star a place in the text and write their prediction about that part in the Response Notes.

Reading the Introduction

Have students read the introductory paragraph. Ask students how they get involved in the story. What tends to happen if they aren't involved?

Reading the Selection

Read the next part of "The Lad" by Jane Yolen, stopping at the bottom of the page. Ask students:
➤ What prediction did the student in this sample lesson make? Do you agree? Why or why not?
➤ After reading this part of the story, what other predictions might you make? Make one that is based on the main character's actions. Make another prediction that pertains to the story line in general.

Remind students to back up their predictions with evidence from the text or their hunches. Point out that most of their predictions will be answered as they continue to read. But even if they are not answered, making predictions keeps readers interested and eager to find out what will happen. Remind students that they can review this page at any time to see how to write predictions.

Question

Before Reading

In this introductory mini-lesson, students learn to ask questions as they read.

BUILDING BACKGROUND

Explain to students that questions arise naturally in the course of reading. Sometimes readers are puzzled because of a character's actions, questions on plot development, or unfamiliar terms. Asking questions is a powerful active reading strategy, because it keeps students focused on what they are reading.

Reading the Introduction

Have students read the introductory paragraph. Ask students: Can you think of other questions you have as you read? Tell them that they will have a chance to record many of their questions in this *Daybook*. Remind students that many questions begin with *Who, What, Where, When, Why,* and *How.*

Reading the Selection

Read the next part of "The Lad" by Jane Yolen, stopping at the bottom of the page. Ask students:
➤ What questions did the reader in the sample ask?
➤ What new questions would you ask, based on your reading?
➤ Can you think of new questions related to this selection that begin with *Who, What, Where, When, Why,* and *How?*

Asking questions is another way to be an active reader. Remind students that asking questions helps keep their interest high. It will also help them complete the activities related to the readings in this *Daybook.*

Apply the Strategies

B e f o r e   R e a d i n g

> **In this mini-lesson, students practice marking up the text, visualizing, predicting, and questioning as they read the rest of the story.**

BUILDING BACKGROUND
Remind students that new skills must be practiced. The active reading skills introduced here can be practiced prior to beginning Unit 1. Tell students to refer back to earlier mini-lessons for options in marking up the text and writing in the Response Notes. In this mini-lesson, students are asked to use at last two strategies discussed in this introduction. Challenge students to use more strategies if possible.

R e a d i n g   t h e   I n t r o d u c t i o n

Read through the introduction with students. Write these four strategies on the board as a reference for students and discuss why each one is important:
➤ Mark up the text
➤ Visualize
➤ Predict
➤ Question

R e a d i n g   t h e   S e l e c t i o n

Read the ending of "The Lad" by Jane Yolen. Ask students:
➤ What words, sentences, or key ideas do you want to keep track of?
➤ What visual images can you keep track of by sketching them in the Response Notes?
➤ What predictions do you have about the main character or the story line?
➤ What questions do you have about the main character, the story, or the ending?

Encourage students to reread the entire story as they make notes to themselves and highlight text as desired. When students finish, allow them to share their responses with the whole class. Tell them they should now consider themselves active readers. Ask students how it felt to be actively involved in their reading. Remind them that they will have further opportunities to practice as they read and respond to the selections in this *Daybook*.

Unit Overview

In this unit, students learn to identify the most important ideas, make inferences based on a character's thoughts and actions, and use what they know to make predictions. Explain to students that these skills will help them be active readers, and that good readers use them to get the most out of their reading.

Reading the Art

Give students a moment to study the artwork. Then have students discuss these questions:

- What three words are part of the art?
- What does each word mean?
- Why might these words be chosen to introduce a unit titled *Reading Well?*

Literature Focus

Lesson	Literature
1. Getting the Big Picture	**Ann Redpath**, from *Why Do We Laugh?*
	This nonfiction selection is about how the element of surprise makes things funny, and about how people laugh differently in different circumstances.
2. Reading into a Story	**Patricia MacLachlan**, from *Sarah, Plain and Tall*
	Young Caleb and his older sister Anna talk about their Mama, who died giving birth to Caleb.
3. Thinking Ahead	**Josepha Sherman**, "Hare, Otter, Monkey, and Badger"
	A group of animals has problems with the goods they steal from a peddler, and the hare tricks everyone else.

Reading Focus

Lesson	Reading Skill
1. Getting the Big Picture	To find main ideas, look for the author's most important points about the subject.
2. Reading into a Story	Use the information the author provides to make inferences about characters' feelings and situations.
3. Thinking Ahead	Making predictions about what will happen next keeps you involved in a story.

Writing Focus

Lesson	Writing Assignment
1. Getting the Big Picture	Write a paragraph about a funny experience you've had, beginning with a main idea and including some details about that idea.
2. Reading into a Story	Write a journal entry from the perspective of Anna or Caleb about one day of living on the prairie farm.
3. Thinking Ahead	Write an ending to the story.

1 Getting the Big Picture

B e f o r e   R e a d i n g

FOCUS
To find main ideas, look for the author's most important points about the subject.

In the lesson, students learn to identify the subject and the most important ideas in a piece of writing.

BUILDING BACKGROUND

Vocabulary Warm-up
Begin the lesson with this **Context Clues** activity. Write these vocabulary words and the sentences that follow on the board. Ask students to define each word, using context clues within the sentences to help them.

weird   reflex   tense   phony   situations

1. It was <u>weird</u> to see everyone in costume when it wasn't Halloween and even stranger that no one seemed to notice. *(An example of something* weird *is given.)*
2. When the doctor taps your kneecap in just the right place, your leg raises in a <u>reflex.</u> It's a response you cannot control. *(The words that follow it explain* reflex.*)*
3. She was so <u>tense</u> before the big game that she couldn't eat or sleep. *(Not eating and sleeping help describe symptoms of being* tense.*)*
4. It is <u>phony</u> to look and act like someone you are not. *(The rest of the sentence explains what* phony *is like.)*
5. Some <u>situations</u>, or events, require fast help. *(A synonym—events—is given.)*

Prereading Strategy
In this selection, students learn about laughing—why we laugh and about different kinds of laughs. Help students prepare for the selection by creating a **Word Web.** Write the word *laugh* in a circle on the board. Write the following questions on the arms of the web:

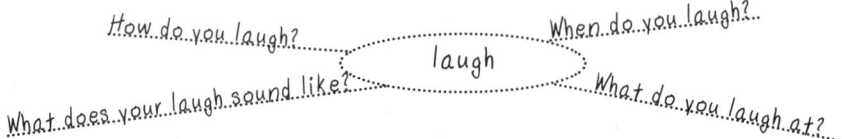

R e a d i n g   t h e   S e l e c t i o n

RESPONSE STRATEGY
Students are to ask questions about the subject and the most important ideas and underline clues to the answers.
Sample Response:
Subject: Why Do We Laugh?
Important idea: An unexpected, weird, funny change makes us laugh.

CRITICAL READING SKILL
Help students find the subject and main ideas in the selection. Often a new paragraph signals a new idea. If students break down the text on page 16 into more than one important idea, help them see that the whole page relates to the idea that we tend to laugh at surprises, and what surprises us changes, depending on our age.

REREADING
After students have read the selection, encourage them to go back and reread it. Make sure they have underlined the subject and the main ideas. Remind students that the title often provides an important clue.

Writing

In this lesson, students create a paragraph with a main idea and sentences that tell about the main idea.

DESCRIBE ONE OF YOUR LAUGHS

Encourage students to use different senses to describe one of their own laughs.

Sample Response:

I hold my breath. My face gets red as a beet. Then a funny sound explodes out of me in little high-pitched squeaks.

LAUGHING

In this activity, students review their underlining in the selection and record each main idea in their own words in the space provided. Remind them that the main ideas answer the questions *when? why?* and *what kind?*

Sample Response:

Idea #1: People laugh when something funny surprises them.
Idea #2: People laugh because it just happens. We don't have to work at it.
Idea #3: There are a lot of different kinds of laughs, like a belly laugh, a scared laugh, and a phony laugh.

Help students see that in Idea #1, using the word "when" in the answer helps them to identify the main idea that answers the question *when?* In Idea #2, the word "because" helps describe a main idea that answers the question *why?* In Idea #3, the question *what kind?* means that examples are part of the main idea.

A FUNNY EXPERIENCE

In this activity, students are to write about a funny experience they've had. Their paragraphs should contain main ideas and sentences that tell about the main ideas. Remind students to begin by completing the sentence "The funniest thing that ever happened to me was...." Encourage them to organize their thoughts. They may start by making notes about two or three ideas they want to include.

Sample Response:

The funniest thing I ever did was to fall off my bike into a big mud puddle. I was on my way to my friend's house. I was riding through some construction when my bike slipped in a big mud puddle. I fell off, and my whole body just slid through the mud like some kind of slip and slide ride! When I got up I looked like I was covered in chocolate. The oozy mud was dripping off the ends of my hair, my nose, and my fingers. Only my eyes were free of mud. There were some workers nearby. They were trying hard not to laugh at me. Finally, I couldn't help myself. I sat down in the middle of the mud and laughed. Then everyone else laughed.

WRITING REMINDERS

As students write their paragraphs, remind them to:

✔ Indent the first sentence in their paragraphs.

✔ Make sure each sentence ends with a period, question mark, or exclamation point.

✔ Follow their outlines or word webs.

Reading into a Story

Before *Reading*

In the lesson, students learn to make inferences about a character's thoughts and feelings based on what the character says and does.

BUILDING BACKGROUND

Vocabulary Warm-up

Introduce students to new words with a **Vocabulary Quiz Show.**

| hearthstones | slab | holler | wretched | prairie |

Begin by writing each of the five words above on a note card. Write the definition for each word on another card. Then pass the ten cards out to ten students in the class. Have a student who holds a word card read it out loud. Help with pronunciation if necessary. Have the student holding the correct card read the definition out loud. Discuss each word and ask students to think of sentences using each word.

Prereading Strategy

Use an **Anticipation Guide** to help students build background to the selection. What do students know about early days and life on the prairie? Present these statements to start students thinking about the selection:

1. Agree   Disagree   The prairie is a rugged, mountain region on the West Coast of the United States.

2. Agree   Disagree   The weather on the prairie provided many challenges for people in the olden days.

3. Agree   Disagree   People living on the prairie in the olden days had many conveniences to help them.

Reading the Selection

RESPONSE STRATEGY

Students are asked to circle or underline important information about Anna and Caleb and record inferences they make in the Response Notes.

Sample Response:

"'Well, Papa doesn't sing anymore,' said Caleb very softly." Inference: Caleb seems sad when he talks about his Papa. He knows that something happened to make Papa not sing anymore. Maybe it has something to do with Mama.

CRITICAL READING SKILL

Remind students to underline important information about each character. Have them try to figure out why the person feels, acts, or thinks the way he or she does. If students have trouble identifying important information about a character, have them begin by looking for clues wherever they find the character's name used.

REREADING

Have students reread the selection, looking for additional information about Caleb and Anna. Remind students that in addition to the words each character speaks in conversation, other clues about each character are embedded in the descriptive text.

W r i t i n g

In this lesson, students write a journal entry from the point of view of Anna or Caleb.

HOW DO YOU FEEL?

Encourage students to think about the selection before they begin to write about how they feel. Remind them to explain why they feel this way, giving an example from the text if desired.

Sample Response:

It made me feel sad, because everyone in the family was sad—Anna, Caleb, and Papa, who doesn't sing anymore. They must be lonely without Mama. Thinking about Caleb never knowing his mother made me the saddest.

INFERENCE CHART

In this activity, students read an inference about Anna and Caleb and then write down information from the story that supports each inference. Have them read the story carefully to find clues. Suggest that students begin by reading their underlining or highlighting. Do they find something that fits?

Sample Response:

Anna feels Caleb is a little responsible for their mother's death. Information from story: "He was homely and plain, and he had a terrible holler and a horrid smell. But these were not the worst of him. Mama died the next morning. That was the worst thing about Caleb."

JOURNAL ENTRY

In this activity, students write a journal entry of one day in the life of Anna or Caleb. Remind students to use character information in the text, along with their inferences, as the basis for their writing. Suggest that they choose a day and create a word web around that day. For example, they might choose "the day Mama died" and add spokes for things to include in the day's events from Anna's point of view. Discuss how writing in first-person voice means that the word "I" is used, as though they are Anna or Caleb.

Sample Response:

(Excerpt from Anna's entry)

When I woke up that morning, I knew something awful was going to happen. Mama had been sick for days. When my brother was finally born, Mama handed him to me. I wanted to hand him right back to her! He was loud and smelly and ugly. But I was glad he was finally here. Now Mama could be well again. I missed her happy voice and singing.

WRITING REMINDERS

As students write their paragraphs, remind them to:

✔ Write in first-person voice.

✔ Make sure each sentence ends with a period, question mark, or exclamation point.

✔ Read the paragraph carefully to make sure they spell each word correctly.

3 Thinking Ahead

Before Reading

In the lesson, students use what they know to predict what will happen next.

BUILDING BACKGROUND

Vocabulary Warm-up

As a warm-up, ask students to complete the **Cloze Sentences** below.

badger   peddler   rejoined   fascinating   sprawling

1. He _____ the party after leaving to go pick up the surprise birthday cake.
2. The dog was _____ all over the floor like a giraffe with all four legs going in different directions.
3. In the old days, people looked forward to visits from the _____, so they could obtain household items they needed.
4. It is _____ to imagine what would happen if Harry Potter went to your school.
5. The clever _____ dug his way through many backyards.

Prereading Strategy

To help students build background, use this **Think-Pair-and-Share** activity.
1. "Look at that," he whispered. "That peddler is carrying his goods with him in that basket."
2. "We could use these goods, my friends."
3. One day, Hare called Otter, Monkey, and Badger to him.
4. "I see a block of salt, a nice mat . . . who knows what else?"
   Pair up students and ask them to discuss these questions:
➤ In what order do you think the sentences should go?
➤ What does the story seem to be about?

Reading the Selection

RESPONSE STRATEGY

Students are asked to stop and predict what will happen at three points in the selection by writing their predictions in the Response Notes and highlighting the information they use to make each prediction.

Sample Response:
They found the block of salt, the woven mat, a small water wheel, and a sack of beans.
What will they do with the things they stole? use them, trade them, or sell them

CRITICAL READING SKILL

Students are asked to predict what will happen next. Help them to gather information from the text much like a detective gathers clues by asking questions.
What's going on? (*Four animals are led by Hare on a path that doesn't seem "right."*)
What doesn't make sense? (*The objects they steal don't seem to be needed by or even useful to the animals.*)
What hunches do I have? (*The other animals will end up teaching Hare a lesson.*)

REREADING

After students have read the selection, encourage them to go back and reread it, making sure they have highlighted the text upon which they based each prediction.

W r i t i n g

In this lesson, students write their own ending for the story.

IT'S A MATCH

In this activity, students describe a prediction that happened.

Sample Response:

I said that the other animals would ask the Hare for help on how to divide up what they stole. I thought he would do it so he got the best stuff, and I was right!

If some students' predictions were all wrong, have them choose one of those instead. They can write about what did happen, and why.

HARE'S MOST CLEVER TRICK

In this activity, students describe Hare's most clever trick and why they think it is the best one.

Sample Response:

Hare was so clever when he stuck bean skins all over his stomach. But, I thought he was doing it so they would think he had chickenpox!

If students have trouble identifying Hare's tricks, have them reread the selection and use a highlighter pen to highlight descriptions of Hare's clever tricks.

WRITE YOUR OWN ENDING

In this activity, students write their own ending for the story. Encourage them to use one of their predictions as the basis for a new ending.

Sample Response:

But just then, the sun came out and warmed Hare's skin. The bean skins began popping off his stomach like little jumping beans.

"You were not telling us the truth!" the other animals cried. "We are not going to listen to you anymore."

First the animals returned the stuff they stole to the peddler. Then they sat down to decide what they should do to Hare. They cooked up a big batch of bean soup and made him eat it all. For three days he really did have a sore stomach.

WRITING REMINDERS

As students write their endings to the story, remind them to:

✔ Indent the first sentence in their paragraphs.

✔ Make sure each sentence ends with a period, question mark, or exclamation point.

✔ Use details from the story that will tie everything together.

READING FICTION

Unit Overview

In this unit, students learn to identify three elements of a fiction story: point of view, setting, and plot. Explain to students that each element plays an important part in the development of a story. Point of view lets the reader know who is telling the story. The setting lets readers know where the story takes place and helps them visualize it. The plot moves the story along and helps readers predict what will happen next. Help students understand that identifying these elements when they read is another way to be an active reader. It helps them get more out of their reading.

Reading the Art

Have students look at the artwork. What elements do they see? Write them on the board. Tell students to imagine that this drawing represents a story illustration. Ask students:

- From whose point of view might this story be told?
- What can you tell about the character from the drawing?
- What is the setting for this story?
- What might a good plot be, based on the elements you see in the drawing?

L i t e r a t u r e   F o c u s

Lesson	Literature
1. Who's Telling the Story?	**Laurence Yep,** from *Later, Gator* Teddy brings an alligator into his family's apartment, and the family reacts to this unexpected surprise.
2. Where Does the Story Take Place?	**E.B. White,** from *Charlotte's Web* The barn where Wilbur the pig lives is described in detail.
3. What Happens?	**Cynthia Rylant,** "A Pet" A girl named Emma is given a goldfish, which she doesn't like at first because she wanted a dog or cat, but which she eventually comes to care about. The goldfish gets sick and eventually dies.

R e a d i n g   F o c u s

Lesson	Reading Skill
1. Who's Telling the Story?	Point of view in a story affects how you "see" events and characters.
2. Where Does the Story Take Place?	When you read a description of a setting, form a picture of the place in your mind.
3. What Happens?	In many stories, the plot centers around problems and how they end up or are resolved.

W r i t i n g   F o c u s

Lesson	Writing Assignment
1. Who's Telling the Story?	Rewrite the scene where Teddy's father discovers the alligator from the father's point of view.
2. Where Does the Story Take Place?	Write a paragraph that uses detailed sensory images to describe your perfect room.
3. What Happens?	Create a plot for a story about a pet, coming up with both a problem and a solution to that problem which you could write a story about.

1 Who's Telling the Story?

Before Reading

FOCUS

Point of view in a story affects how you "see" events and characters.

In the lesson, students learn about point of view as they predict how characters will react.

BUILDING BACKGROUND

Vocabulary Warm-up

To introduce new vocabulary words to students, use this **Matching Definitions** activity. Write the words and definitions in two columns on the board. Ask students to match them up by drawing a line between the word in the left column and its definition in the right column. For added practice, ask students to think of a sentence for each word.

1. *herbalists*   settled down, diminished
2. *slithering*   a long pointy nose of many animals
3. *surge*   people who collect, grow, or heal using herbs
4. *snout*   slinking or sliding along like a snake
5. *subsided*   a sudden, powerful movement

Prereading Strategy

Introduce this selection with this whole-class **Previewing** activity. Have students quickly skim the introduction and first three paragraphs of the story to gain background information.

1. Where does this story take place? *(Chinatown in San Francisco)*
2. Who is telling the story? *(the older brother, Teddy)*
3. What do you think the story is about? *(an alligator that Teddy brings home.)*
4. What do you think will happen? *(the alligator will escape in the apartment)*

Reading the Selection

RESPONSE STRATEGY

Students are to make predictions by jotting down their thoughts in the Response Notes. Have students underline information in the text and then make notes about other members of the family as one basis for making predictions.

   Sample Response:

"*Mama kept a can of pine scent by the doorway because of Mr. Wong.*"
Prediction: *Mama knows how to take care of most things, but an alligator? I think she will be very mad at Teddy!*

CRITICAL READING SKILL

Remind students to look for clues as to how other family members will respond. Clues can appear as reactions of family members or as Teddy's thoughts or dialogue.

"*The alligator hadn't looked nearly so big in the department store.*"
Prediction: *(The alligator is bigger than Teddy thought. If Teddy is a little scared, then probably other family members will be, too.)*

REREADING

Have students reread the selection to see if they can find any more clues to how other family members will respond.

W r i t i n g

QUICK ASSESS

Do students' endings:

✓ seem logical?

✓ build on details from the story?

✓ present the ending from Father's point of view?

In this lesson, students rewrite the last scene of the story from the father's point of view.

PREDICT TEDDY'S FATHER'S REACTION

In this activity, students predict how Teddy's father will respond to the alligator.

Sample Response:

Father was tired when he came home. He looked at me and knew something was funny. When he saw the alligator, he stopped and stared at it and then at me. I never saw him look at me like that before. He didn't have to say a word. I picked up the alligator and put it back in the box.

Encourage students to be creative in their responses. Have them imagine what Mr. Wong might have looked like, said, and done when he saw the alligator and to describe his reactions in detail.

YOUR FAMILY'S REACTION

In this activity, students predict their family's response if they were to bring home an alligator.

Sample Response:

You could hear my dad yell at me all the way down the block. My sister Emma googled, but she is only three months old. My brother Pete thought it was cool and wanted to take it to school. But my mom was a surprise. "Look at him!" she said sweetly. He seemed to like her, because he stopped jumping around and crawled up next to her. We all just sat there watching. We were afraid to say a word.

FATHER'S POINT OF VIEW

In this activity, students rewrite the ending for the story, this time from Father's point of view.

Sample Response:

"Bobby! Will SOMEONE tell me what this alligator is doing in the bathtub? I will give you five seconds to tell me before I put you all in there with him!"

I was mad. I got scared when I saw the alligator in the bathtub. I didn't think it was funny at all.

WRITING REMINDERS

As students write their endings to the story, remind them to:

✓ Indent the first sentence in their paragraphs.

✓ Make sure each sentence ends with a period, question mark, or exclamation point.

✓ Write from Father's point of view.

 **Where Does the Story Take Place?**

B e f o r e   R e a d i n g

FOCUS

When you read a description of a setting, form a picture of the place in your mind.

In the lesson, students learn how descriptions of sights, sounds, and smells create the setting for a piece of writing.

BUILDING BACKGROUND

Vocabulary Warm-up

These vocabulary words may be unfamiliar to students. Introduce them by organizing a **Vocabulary Quiz Show.**

    perspiration   loft   stalls   grindstones   scythes

Write each word on a note card and the definition for each word on another card, then give the ten cards to ten different students in class. Ask a student with a word card to read it out loud. Help with pronunciation if necessary. Have the student with the matching definition card read it out loud and discuss each word in the context of a barn. Then ask students to think of sentences using each word.

Prereading Strategy

The setting for this selection is a farm. Help students prepare to read by creating a **Word Web.** Write the word *farm* in a circle on the board. Write the following questions on the arms of the web. Encourage students to add one more arm with a new question if desired.

What animals can be found on farms?   What activities take place on a farm?

What buildings are part of many farms?   *farm*   What would you do if you lived on a farm?

R e a d i n g   t h e   S e l e c t i o n

RESPONSE STRATEGY

Students are to identify phrases that describe the smells and sights of the barn. Encourage them to highlight the phrases in two different-colored highlighters or have them jot down "smell" or "sound" in the Response Notes.

Sample Response:

smells: hay, manure, perspiration of tired horses, cow breath; sights: large barn, tired horses, patient cows, cat given a fish-head, wide open barn doors

CRITICAL READING SKILL

Remind students to picture each sentence as they read. It will help them to distinguish between descriptions of sights and those of smells, since they will have difficulty forming an image of a smell. If students still have trouble, have them look for the words "smell" or "smelled" as clues. Encourage students to sketch several sight descriptions in the Response Notes.

REREADING

When students reread the selection, have them pay special attention to how E.B. White sets the scene for the story and introduces one of the main characters, Wilbur. By the time he mentions Wilbur, we know his home. Ask students:

➤ How does knowing first what the barn looks like help our understanding of the rest of the story?

➤ Why do you think he chose to describe the barn before introducing Wilbur?

Writing

In this lesson, students write descriptions of their perfect rooms.

SKETCH THE BARN

In this activity, students draw the barn as they see it in their minds, using details from the story and new details they want to add.

Remind students that when an author creates an image of a place, it does not have to stop with the details provided. Readers are free to add new details of their own.

Sample Response:

OLD BARN

In this activity, students list the smells and sights on a chart.

Sample Response:

Sights	Smells
Wilbur	manure
ladders	hay
milk pails	perspiration from horses
cows	sweet cow breath
perspiring horses	rubber boots

Encourage students to be detectives as they go back and search for more examples to add to their charts.

MY PERFECT ROOM

In this activity, students write their own descriptions of their own perfect rooms. Have students begin by creating word webs or charts listing some of the sights, smells, sounds, and feelings they associate with these perfect spaces.

Encourage students to follow their outlines or word webs as they write, but to feel free to add or subtract items at any time. Remind them to make their descriptions as vivid as possible, so readers can really imagine themselves in the rooms described.

Sample Response:

My perfect room has all of my sports stuff in it. In one corner are bats and baseballs. A basketball hoop is on my bed, and the basketball beside it. My soccer ball is under the bed. My football and uniform are in the closet, and my tennis racket is on the floor with some tennis balls. My perfect room has all the stuff I need for the sports I play.

WRITING REMINDERS

As students write their paragraphs, remind them to:

✔ Include descriptions of sights, sounds, smells, and feelings.

✔ Be creative in their descriptions.

✔ Make sure each sentence ends with a period, question mark, or exclamation point.

3 What Happens?

B e f o r e | *R e a d i n g*

FOCUS

In many stories, the plot centers around problems and how they end up or are resolved.

In the lesson, students learn how the action in a story is centered around the plot.

BUILDING BACKGROUND

Vocabulary Warm-up

Introduce new vocabulary words for this story using **Context Clues.**

relented   viola   debate   ruefully   lolled

1. Jacob's parents finally <u>relented</u>, giving in and buying him the keyboard he had wanted for a year. *(A synonym, giving in, provides a clue.)*
2. She <u>lolled</u> around so long that she had to hurry up to avoid being late for school. *(The situation described gives a clue to the meaning.)*
3. He listened to the candidates <u>debate</u> the issue, but in the end he still couldn't choose which arguments to support. *(A definition of the word is in the sentence.)*
4. Mikka played <u>viola</u> in the string orchestra until she decided she wanted a lower pitched instrument and took up the cello instead. *(The description gives a clue as to the meaning.)*
5. She <u>ruefully</u> mailed the invitations, deeply regretful that she hadn't done it earlier. *(A synonym, deeply regretful, is in the sentence.)*

Prereading Strategy

Build students' background to the selection with an **Anticipation Guide.** Present these sentences to get them thinking about goldfish and aquariums.

1. Agree   Disagree   Goldfish are always orange.
2. Agree   Disagree   Goldfish don't live more than a few days in an aquarium.
3. Agree   Disagree   A goldfish can be a good pet.

R e a d i n g   t h e   S e l e c t i o n

RESPONSE STRATEGY

Students are asked to identify Emma's problems as a way to see how those problems move along the plot of the story. Have students circle Emma's problems and then write in the Response Notes what they think will happen.

Sample Response:

Joshua seems to be sick. Prediction: I think Joshua is dying.

CRITICAL READING SKILL

Ask students to review the problems they marked in the text. Which ones were solved and which ones weren't? Ask students questions about the problems.

To move the plot along, do all problems have to be solved? *(No, sometimes the plot moves along because the character must think of another way to deal with the problem.)*

How does the plot continue if a problem is not solved? *(The character may be challenged to do something different or to think about the situation in a new way.)*

REREADING

Have students reread the story as they consider carefully Emma's problems. Remind students that a problem can revolve around how to *feel* as well as what to *do*. Ask students how they would describe Emma's final problem at the end of the story.

Writing

In this lesson, students write their own plots for a story.

PREDICT AND REACT

In this activity, students compare their predictions with what really happened. Encourage students to reread the story and then review their predictions before writing.

Sample Response:

I thought she would be mad in the beginning that her parents gave her a stupid fish, but she wasn't. Maybe it was because he had a name. I also didn't think that Joshua would die, even though he was old. I didn't want him to, because I know how sad it is. The ending made me cry, because it reminded me of when my dog died.

PLOT MAP

In this activity, students work with three problems and how each one is resolved. Encourage them to review the story and their notes to find the solution to each problem. If students have trouble identifying a solution, have them ask these questions:
What happens next? What does Emma do?

Sample Response:

Problem: Emma wants a pet, but her parents don't want her to have one. Solution: They decide to get her a goldfish. I think because goldfish don't shed, scratch, or need walks or a fenced-in yard.

MY STORY

Students write their own plots for a story about a pet. Have them brainstorm or create word webs to help them arrive at problems and solutions they like. Some students may want to develop their problem-and-solution plot maps into stories.

Sample Response:

Raymond was Jen's very special rabbit. But Raymond kept getting out of any hutch he was in. One day Jen's neighbor, a policeman, brought him home in his patrol car! Jen said Raymond had magical powers, but her parents didn't see it that way. They said she had to give him away. It made her cry to think of it. Solution: Jen's mom's friend is a kindergarten teacher. When she heard about Raymond, she said, "Let me take him! That way Jen can come see him and Raymond can have lots of children to love him and take care of him." So now Raymond freely hops around Room 6 in Jen's old school.

WRITING REMINDERS

As students write their story plots, remind them to:

✔ Describe the pets.

✔ Describe the problems and solutions in detail.

✔ Make sure the solutions are logical and interesting.

UNDERSTANDING LANGUAGE

Unit Overview

In this unit, students look at how authors use descriptive language, metaphors, exaggerations, and similes. Descriptive language uses words and details to create pictures. Metaphors make comparisons between two things, which help readers to understand ideas. Exaggerations stretch the truth for emphasis or purely for fun, and similes compare two things using *like* or *as*. Help students see that using these elements in their writing helps bring characters, settings, and plots to life for readers.

Reading the Art

Have students look at the artwork. What do they see? Write students' ideas on the board. Tell students to look at this drawing as a book illustration. Ask students:

- Who might be characters in the story?
- What is the setting for the story?
- Do you think the book is fiction or nonfiction, and why?
- If the drawing were not in the book, how would you describe it so that readers could see it in their minds?

UNDERSTANDING LANGUAGE

Literature Focus

Lesson	Literature
1. Creating Pictures with Words	**Gary Paulsen**, from *Cookcamp*
	A boy and his grandmother serve food to a group of workmen. The boy is fascinated by the actions of the men.
2. Comparing One Thing to Another	**Langston Hughes**, "Dreams";
	Andreya Renee Allen, "Black Is Beautiful";
	Brandon N. Johnson, "Black Ancestors"
	These three poems focus on the shared history, traditions, pride, and dreams of black people.
3. Stretching the Truth	**Mary Pope Osborne**, from *Davy Crockett*
	This is a tall tale about Davy Crockett that uses exaggeration and similes to demonstrate what kind of man Crockett was. It focuses on his wrestling the Big Eater, a huge panther who wants to eat him.

Reading Focus

Lesson	Reading Skill
1. Creating Pictures with Words	When you read descriptive words and details, try to picture the character or scene in your mind.
2. Comparing One Thing to Another	When you read a metaphor, think about how the two things being compared are alike or what the comparison suggests.
3. Stretching the Truth	As you read, notice the way authors use similes or exaggeration to emphasize an idea or add humor.

Writing Focus

Lesson	Writing Assignment
1. Creating Pictures with Words	Write a description of your school cafeteria, focusing on including sensory details and words.
2. Comparing One Thing to Another	Write a short poem, using comparison, about something you value and care about.
3. Stretching the Truth	Construct a web with two similes and two exaggerations that describe a subject you choose.

Creating Pictures with Words

B e f o r e   R e a d i n g

FOCUS

When you read descriptive words and details, try to picture the character or scene in your mind.

In the lesson, students learn how descriptive language helps readers picture a scene in their minds.

BUILDING BACKGROUND

Vocabulary Warm-up

Make sure students are familiar with the words in this lesson by completing these **Cloze Sentences**. Write the five words and sentences below on the board. Have student volunteers read the sentences with the correct words added. Let students make up new sentences for each word.

dare	arranged	sugar lumps	soaked	crumble

1. In a library, fiction books are _____ in alphabetical order by the author's last name.
2. Due to erosion, the hillside began to _____, making it unsafe to build there.
3. Don't you _____ borrow my bike without asking!
4. By the time he grabbed a towel, the paint had already _____ into the rug.
5. Restaurants rarely offer _____ to put in coffee anymore.

Prereading Strategy

Prepare students to read this selection with this **Think-Pair-and-Share** activity. Write these four sentences on the board:

1. "The men will be in soon and they will be hungry."
2. "He wanted them to be done because he had about a thousand questions to ask his grandmother."
3. "Now help me set the tables before they get here."
4. "After they eat maybe you can ask them the question about how bad things can make good things."

Divide the class into pairs. Ask each pair of students to discuss what the correct order of sentences is. (*1, 3, 4, 2.*)

R e a d i n g   t h e   S e l e c t i o n

RESPONSE STRATEGY

Students are asked to underline the words and details Paulsen uses to create vivid pictures in readers' minds.

Sample Response:

"They were so huge as they came in that he couldn't help moving in back of his grandmother's dress until they were all seated."

CRITICAL READING SKILL

Ask students to read the selection one paragraph at a time, underlining at least 2 words or details in each paragraph.

REREADING

Have students reread this story to find even more details about the story. Ask students to underline vivid words and phrases, such as "lump" or "strips of bacon."

W r i t i n g

Do students' descriptions:

✓ include information from their brainstormed lists?

✓ include descriptions of sights, sounds, and smells?

✓ show creativity?

In this lesson, students write a description of their school cafeteria.

FAVORITE DESCRIPTION

In this activity, students choose their favorite descriptive sentences in the selection. Then they draw sketches of the pictures they see in their minds.

Sample Response:

"It looked so strange to him, their huge fingers holding the tiny sugar lumps in each cup like little toys."

Remind students that they do not have to draw the image perfectly. They only have to capture the *feeling* of what they see in their minds.

SCHOOL CAFETERIA BRAINSTORM

In this activity, students brainstorm what it is like eating lunch in the cafeteria. Encourage students to use word webs to brainstorm. The arms might have these headings:

(macaroni and cheese, corn dogs, spilled milk, some girl's perfume) ······ **Smells**

(kids standing in line, groups of kids sitting at tables, eating and talking, one person sitting alone, crying, two kids arguing, the principal)

Sights

(cafeteria)

(two kids shouting, the crunch of someone eating chips, the clang of trays, balls bouncing, laughing, the teacher asking kids to be quieter) ····· **Sounds** ······

SCHOOL CAFETERIA DESCRIPTION

Students write a description of the cafeteria, using sensory details and descriptions from their brainstormed lists. Remind students that they do not have to use everything on their lists. Encourage students not merely to list items, but to describe each of them in detail so they are truly painting vivid pictures for readers.

Sample Response:

Walking into the lunch room would make my mom's knees shake. It is very noisy. But for me and my friends, it's life. In one corner kids are playing chess. They always bring weird sandwiches from home. The lunch line is long. A dog wanders in off the playground. Some kids feed him and hide him under a table, but he barks. A teacher leads him outside again. A little kid drops a toy in the trash can and is crying. The usual trading of desserts goes on. Today I want to find my best friend and sit quietly, wishing I were somewhere else instead of in this small, hot lunch room.

WRITING REMINDERS

As students write their descriptions, remind them to:

✓ Refer to their brainstorm boxes on page 48 for ideas.

✓ Include descriptions of what they see, hear, and smell.

✓ Indent the first sentence in their paragraphs.

 **Comparing One Thing to Another**

B e f o r e | *R e a d i n g*

FOCUS

When you read a metaphor, think about how the two things being compared are alike or what the comparison suggests.

In the lesson, students learn how to use metaphors to compare one thing to another.

BUILDING BACKGROUND

Vocabulary Warm-up

Help students prepare for the lesson with this **Matching Definitions** activity. Write the words/phrases and definitions in two columns on the board. Ask students to match up a word with its definition by drawing a line between the word in the left column and its definition in the right column.

1. *hold fast* — measure up
2. *barren* — fearlessness, confidence
3. *compete* — cling tightly to
4. *ancestors* — desolate, with little or no vegetation
5. *boldness* — ones who go before, forebears

Prereading Strategy

Introduce the lesson with this **Previewing** activity. Have students quickly look over each poem.

1. What is the first poem about? *(dreams)*
2. What color is the subject of the second poem? *(black)*
3. What does the third poem talk about? *(freedom, black people, boldness)*
4. What do you think all of these poems have in common? *(I think they are all about black people, being strong, and feeling good about yourself. But they make you think, even if you aren't black.)*

R e a d i n g   t h e   S e l e c t i o n

RESPONSE STRATEGY

Students are asked to highlight the comparisons they find in each poem and record how these comparisons make them feel in the Response Notes.

Sample Response:

Life is a broken-winged bird; Life is a barren field; I could feel how sad it is when your dreams die.

CRITICAL READING SKILL

Ask students to read over the metaphors they marked in the text. Remind them to make notes about how each one made them feel in the Response Notes. *(Example: Black is boldness. It reminds me of what my mom and dad always tell me. It makes me feel proud.)*

   If students have trouble identifying the comparisons in each poem, have them look for the word *is* to help them. Remind students that metaphors help readers get a clearer picture of what is being described.

REREADING

Ask students to read each poem again and to write a sentence about how each poem makes them feel in the Response Notes. Tell them that the power of using metaphors helps readers feel and experience ideas and images vividly and deeply.

W r i t i n g

In this lesson, students write a short poem about something they value.

WHICH POEM DO YOU LIKE BEST?

In this activity, students explain which poem they like best, and why. To help students choose their favorite poem, have them read back over their notes and the comparisons they marked, along with their comments. Have them ask themselves these questions:

➤ Which comparisons create the strongest images for me?

➤ Which poem makes me feel something deeply or reminds me of something?

Sample Response:

What poem I like best: "Dreams".

Why I like it the best: The poet makes me want to fight to make sure my dream of becoming a dancer doesn't die.

ANSWER THE QUESTIONS

In this activity, students answer questions related to three metaphors. Encourage students to read back over each poem before they answer the questions. Give students time to share their answers in a whole-class discussion.

Sample Response:

How is a life without dreams like a frozen field? You just feel empty, like there is nothing inside. There is no happiness, nothing to look forward to. You are unable to move.

BRAINSTORM THINGS OF VALUE

Students brainstorm things that are meaningful to them in preparation for writing poems. Remind them that in brainstorming it's important to think of as many things as possible. Creating word webs may help some students.

Sample Response:

my dog, my parents, piano, love, my best friend, my grandma, the beach

A POEM

In this activity, students choose one thing from their brainstormed lists. Then they think of something to compare it to and use that metaphor in short poems. Create several examples to do with the whole class before having students work on their own. Some students will have trouble thinking of comparisons. Have them ask: What does this object remind me of? Love reminds me of wind, a snake, tears. What does it make me feel like? "frisky, sad, warm"

Sample Response:

Love is the wind, frisking through my hair. It is snaky, winding its way up from my toes. It is like tears when my friend moves away. It is warm when I go to sleep in the back seat on a trip and hear the rain and the windshield wipers slapping the message, "I love you, I love you."

WRITING REMINDERS

As students write their poems, remind them to:

✓ Choose something they value from their brainstormed lists.

✓ Compare those items with something else.

✓ Use the metaphors in their poems.

 **Stretching the Truth**

B e f o r e | *R e a d i n g*

FOCUS

As you read, notice the way authors use similes or exaggeration to emphasize an idea or to add humor.

In the lesson, students learn to identify exaggeration and similes, two ways to add interest and fun to a piece of writing.

BUILDING BACKGROUND

Vocabulary Warm-up

Prepare students to read this tall tale with this **Context Clues** activity. Write these vocabulary words and the sentences that follow on the board. Ask students to define each word, using clues within the sentence to help them arrive at the meaning.

> *extraordinary   fox fire   varmint   brag   thicket*

1. He liked to <u>brag</u> about how strong he was, but the boasting stopped when his little sister beat him at arm wrestling. (*Boasting is a synonym for* brag.)
2. The <u>varmint</u> wouldn't leave them alone; the animal pestered everyone in a ten-mile radius. (*From the sentence we know a* varmint *is a pesky animal.*)
3. The dense growth of the <u>thicket</u> made it a safe place for animals to hide. (*The synonym, dense growth, is a clue.*)
4. Seeing the aurora borealis was the most amazing, astonishing, <u>extraordinary</u> night of her life. (*Amazing and astonishing are synonyms for* extraordinary.)
5. The ball of <u>fox fire</u> lit up the decaying wood, casting an eerie glow into the darkening sky. (*The sentence explains the meaning of* fox fire.)

Prereading Strategy

Help students build background to the selection with this **Anticipation Guide**. Present these statements to get students started thinking about tall tales.

1. Agree   Disagree   Tall tales are a good way of learning about history.
2. Agree   Disagree   Tall tales often tell about people in history.
3. Agree   Disagree   In tall tales, people, animals, and even the weather can be exaggerated!

R e a d i n g   t h e   S e l e c t i o n

RESPONSE STRATEGY

Students are asked to underline examples of exaggeration and simile. Remind students that similes contain the words *like* and *as*. Exaggerations are statements that are enlarged beyond the truth.

Sample Response:

Simile: <u>Anyone could see that he walked like an ox, ran like a fox, and swam like an eel.</u> Exaggeration: <u>Davy . . . could carry thunder in his fist.</u>

CRITICAL READING SKILL

Go over examples of exaggeration and simile in the lesson. Then find one example of each in the selection. (*For example: "When I was a baby, my cradle was the shell of a six-hundred-pound turtle!" [exaggeration]; "Davy neighed like a horse, then hollered like a screech owl." [simile]*)

REREADING

Ask students to reread the selection for more examples. Remind them to note in the Response Notes whether each comparison is an exaggeration, a simile, or both.

Writing

In this lesson, students think of two similes and two exaggerations to use in writing their own tall tales.

WHAT I ENJOYED MOST

In this activity, students describe what they liked most about the tall tale.

Sample Response:

I liked the part where Davy Crockett fights with the panther. It's funny because he talks to the panther like when he says "Wanna sing a duet?"

Encourage students to include a short example from the story when they describe the parts they liked best.

FAVORITE EXAGGERATION AND SIMILE

In this activity, students write their favorite exaggerations and similes from the story. If they starred their favorites, all they need to do is copy those sentences. If not, have them go back and read all the similes and exaggerations they underlined or highlighted.

Sample Response:

Favorite simile: "He was just sitting there with a pile of bones and skulls all around him like pumpkins in a pumpkin patch." Favorite exaggeration: "Before Davy could beg the varmint's pardon, the panther spit a sea of froth at him, and his teeth began to grind like a sixty-horsepower sawmill."

PLAN A TALL TALE

In this activity, students plan tall tales about people they consider heroes. Have them begin by selecting heroes. They could be people in their families, book characters, or famous people. After choosing the subjects of the tall tales, have students brainstorm characteristics of their heroes. For example, are they honest, smart, artistic, beautiful? Explain that once they have lists of qualities, they can begin to write similes and exaggerations based on them.

Sample Response:

Subject: Mom; Quality: Good with computers; Simile: "My mom's fingers fly across the computer keyboard like a whirlwind." Or, Subject: My cousin Matt; Quality: Really tall: Exaggeration: "My cousin Matt is so tall that clouds bump into his head."

Encourage students to use their notes to write their tall tales.

WRITING REMINDERS

As students plan their tall tales, remind them to:

✔ Choose heroes as their subjects.

✔ Brainstorm lists of qualities about their heroes.

✔ Make sure their two similes and exaggerations reflect qualities on their brainstormed lists.

For use with page 59

Unit Overview

In this unit, students look at how author Roald Dahl uses humor and imagination to bring his characters and scenes to life. In some books he creates a fantasy with enough real-life elements to bring readers into the story. Other times he uses humor or descriptive language. Point out to students that good readers study and then practice the techniques famous authors use. Using fantasy, humor, or descriptive language also provides an effective way to draw readers into the characters, plot, and setting of a story.

Reading the Art

Have students look at the artwork. What elements do they see? Write their ideas on the board. Ask students:

- What is the significance of the hand? Whose hand is it?
- What is the meaning of the rabbit, lightning, and bird, and what is the special significance of the eye?
- How does this illustration help introduce the subject of this unit?
- What books have you read that use tricks, jokes, riddles, and fantasy to help engage readers' interest?

UNDERSTANDING LANGUAGE

Literature Focus

Lesson	Literature
1. A World of Make-Believe	**Roald Dahl**, from *The BFG* This fantasy selection is about a girl named Sophie watching a giant walk down her street in the middle of the night, and about the way that the giant acts.
2. Writing for Laughs	**Roald Dahl**, from *The Twits* Mrs. Twit and Mr. Twit are a couple who like to play nasty jokes on each other. In this selection, Mrs. Twit cooks Mr. Twit spaghetti with worms instead of noodles, and doesn't tell him until he's already finished that he's been eating worms.
3. Picturing a Magical Place	**Roald Dahl**, from *Charlie and the Chocolate Factory* Mr. Wonka gives a tour of his extraordinary chocolate factory, and points out all of the amazing sights.

Reading Focus

Lesson	Reading Skill
1. A World of Make-Believe	Part of the fun in reading a fantasy comes from sharing in the author's wild imaginings.
2. Writing for Laughs	Authors use humor to entertain readers.
3. Picturing a Magical Place	Writers use descriptive language to create pictures in the minds of readers.

Writing Focus

Lesson	Writing Assignment
1. A World of Make-Believe	Write a story about what sort of dreams you would bring to children if you were the giant in the story.
2. Writing for Laughs	Write an opinion paragraph about whether you think Dahl's work is too mean-spirited.
3. Picturing a Magical Place	Write a descriptive paragraph about a popcorn room, in the same fantastic manner that Dahl writes about the chocolate factory.

A World of Make-Believe

Before Reading

FOCUS
Part of the fun in reading a fantasy comes from sharing in the author's wild imaginings.

In the lesson, students learn to identify fantasy and real-life parts of a story.

BUILDING BACKGROUND

Vocabulary Warm-up

Some words in this selection may be unfamiliar. One way to introduce students to them is to organize a **Vocabulary Quiz Show.**

> *shadowy   spurts   peer   cloak   greengrocer*

Write each of the five words on a note card. Write the definitions for each one on another card. Then, pass the ten cards out to ten students. Have a student read one of the word cards out loud. Help with pronunciation if necessary. Ask the student with the matching definition card to read it aloud and discuss each word. Ask students to think of sentences using each word.

Prereading Strategy

Help students gain background for the selection with this **Previewing** activity. Have them read over the first four paragraphs quickly and then answer these questions:
1. What does this story seem to be about? *(a nightmare or scary story)*
2. What characters are in the story? *(Sophie and a giant figure)*
3. Where does it take place? *(on a street in an ordinary neighborhood)*
4. What do you think will happen? *(the figure will come to Sophie's house)*
Ask students to explain the reasons behind their predictions. They may be based on clues found in the first four paragraphs or hunches they have.

Reading the Selection

RESPONSE STRATEGY

Students identify in the Response Notes the parts of the selection that are make-believe and those that are real life.

Sample Response:

It was four times as tall as the tallest human. (MB – make-believe);
Her throat, like her whole body, was frozen with fright. (RL – real life)

CRITICAL READING SKILL

Explain to students that many skillful writers blend fantasy and real life. Some writers create a story that has a believable main character and setting, like Dahl does. Then, Dahl adds make-believe elements. Tell students that sometimes it is difficult to tell when something is fantasy or real life. To determine whether something could happen in real life, ask students to consider not only their own personal experience, but other people's as well. For example, students may say that *they* have never opened their mouths to scream and had no sound come out; however, it is possible for that to happen to someone else.

REREADING

Have students reread the selection. As they read, have them double-check the RL and MB notations they made and add any new ones they may have missed. Remind them that, rather than marking each sentence, they can mark the text in chunks of several sentences, paragraphs, or several paragraphs.

W r i t i n g

Do students' dreams:

✓ include at least one real life and one fantasy element?

✓ seem to be ones a friendly giant would bring?

✓ reflect the giant's point of view?

In this lesson, students write about the dreams of a friendly giant who brings dreams to children.

WHAT WOULD YOU DO?

In this activity, students describe what they would do if they were Sophie.

Sample Response:

If I were Sophie, I would wake myself up so I wouldn't have this dream anymore!

Encourage students to review the selection to see what they can learn about Sophie. Ask them to describe what they would do if they were Sophie, based on information from the text as well as their own hunches.

REAL VERSUS MAKE-BELIEVE

In this activity, students use a chart to list the parts of *The BFG* that seemed real and the parts they had trouble believing. For example:

What parts *seemed* real?	Which parts did you have the most trouble believing?
being afraid	the very long, thin trumpet
Sophie trying to figure out stuff	when the Giant blows whoof through the trumpet

Encourage students to refer to their Response Notes and add new examples if necessary. Ask them to be prepared to give reasons for their answers.

A GIANT'S DREAM TO SLEEPING CHILDREN

In this activity, students envision they are friendly giants who bring dreams to sleeping children. Ask students:

➤ To whom would you bring the dream?

➤ What kind of dream might that child have?

➤ What fantasy and real life elements will you include in your writing?

Remind students to write in first-person voice, since they are friendly giants. Encourage students to use word webs to help brainstorm what they want to include in their stories.

Sample Response:

The giant held the box close to her body. I was scared she would lose it if she didn't, especially in such a big storm. Finally, she sat down in a spot out of the wind and rain and opened the box. Inside were the dreams of many children. She picked up one dream labeled "Carl." Very quietly, she put that dream in her pocket and headed down the street to my house. I was sleeping. I had no idea what was about to happen.

WRITING REMINDERS

As students plan their writing about dreams, remind them to:

✓ Make sure they create dreams that a friendly giant would bring.

✓ Write in first-person voice from the point of view of the giant.

✓ Try to include at least one real life and one fantasy element in their writing.

2 Writing for Laughs

B e f o r e   R e a d i n g

In the lesson, students learn about humor in writing.

BUILDING BACKGROUND

Vocabulary Warm-up

To make sure students understand the vocabulary words below, ask them to complete the five **Cloze Sentences** that follow.

spaghetti   shoveling   squishy   distinctly   bitter

1. By the time the two-year-old finished eating his _____, there was more on him, the walls, the floor, and on the dog than in his stomach.
2. The mud felt oozy and _____ between her toes.
3. One of my winter jobs is _____ snow from our sidewalk and at my grandma's.
4. I didn't win the prize even though my project was best, but, hey, I'm not _____.
5. It was _____ unpleasant to share the tent with someone who snored.

Prereading Strategy

Use this **Think-Pair-and-Share** activity to help students predict what they will read in this selection. Divide the class into pairs. Ask students to read these sentences and discuss the questions that follow.

1. "It gave her great pleasure to watch him eating worms."
2. "The next day, to pay Mr. Twit back for the frog trick, Mrs. Twit sneaked out into the garden and dug up some worms."
3. "'Hey, my spaghetti's moving!' cried Mr. Twit, poking around in it with his fork."
   ➢ What action is taking place? (*Mrs. Twit is going to play a trick on her husband.*)
   ➢ In what order do you think these sentences will appear in the story? (*2, 3, 1.*)
   ➢ Ask students to explain the reasons for their prediction. (*I think that because he played a frog trick on her, they seem to have fun playing tricks on each other.*)

R e a d i n g   t h e   S e l e c t i o n

RESPONSE STRATEGY

Students are asked to highlight the parts of the story that they find funny and to explain the reasons why in the Response Notes.

Sample Response:

"Hey, my spaghetti's moving!" cried Mr. Twit, poking around in it with his fork. This was funny because I could imagine him poking in his spaghetti!

CRITICAL READING SKILL

Ask students to read over the humorous places they marked in the text. Remind them to make notes about why they think each underlined part is funny. Encourage students to share and discuss the types of humor they find.

➢ Is it silly or maybe a little bit wicked?
➢ Is the passage funny because of what a character *says*?
➢ Does the author describe an event in a funny way?

REREADING

Ask students to read the selection again, marking other humor parts they find or that they learned about from discussing the story with their classmates.

W r i t i n g

In this lesson, students write short essays, explaining what they think of Dahl's sense of humor.

HOW WOULD YOU RESPOND?

In this activity, students describe how they would respond if they were Mr. Twit.

Sample Response:

If I were Mr. Twit, I would be thinking of something I could do to really get back at Mrs. Twit for playing such a mean trick on me! (For example, I think I would play a trick on her that would take her by surprise as she cleaned the house. It might involve a mouse.)

MEAN OR FUNNY?

In this activity, students discuss their opinions of Dahl's sense of humor. Explain to students that in this type of writing, it is important to outline the points they want to make. Encourage students to make word webs to help them think about Dahl's sense of humor. For each point they make, have them think of a specific example.

Sample Response:

I think Dahl's humor is very funny and not mean, because it doesn't hurt anyone. Maybe some people think it's mean that Mrs. Twit plays such a mean trick on Mr. Twit, or that she "rocks with horrible laughter" at the end. But I think he probably plays the same kind of tricks on her, and they both seem to like it. They are both a little wicked (like when he wipes his mouth on the tablecloth). Those details make the story even funnier.

WRITING REMINDERS

As students plan their writing, remind them to:

✔ Outline the points they want to make.

✔ Give an example for each point.

✔ Make each new idea a new paragraph.

3 Picturing a Magical Place

Before Reading

FOCUS

Writers use descriptive language to create pictures in the minds of readers.

In the lesson, students learn how descriptive language creates pictures in the minds of readers.

BUILDING BACKGROUND

Vocabulary Warm-up

To help students learn words from this selection, use this **Matching Definitions** activity. Write the five words below and their definitions in two columns on the board. Ask students to match them by drawing a line between the word in the left column and its definition in the right column.

1. *churning*   surprised; dumbfounded
2. *froth*   stirred up as with a violent motion
3. *rhododendrons*   a purple, violet, lilac color
4. *mauve*   bubbles; foamy liquid
5. *flabbergasted*   flowering plants

Prereading Strategy

Help students gain background for the selection with this **Previewing** activity. To begin, ask students to read quickly the title and first paragraph of the story. Then ask them to answer these four questions, based on their initial reading:

1. What kind of factory does Mr. Wonka own? (*a chocolate factory*)
2. What is he most worried about? (*He worries about the children getting too excited.*)
3. What makes the room so special? (*Mr. Wonka says it is the heart of the whole business.*)
4. What do you think will happen in this room? (*I think it's where the best candy is made. I think one of the children will accidentally break something or maybe sneak a piece of the candy, since Mr. Wonka is so worried.*)

Reading the Selection

RESPONSE STRATEGY

Students underline words and details that help them to create pictures of the scene in their minds.

Sample Response:

There were green meadows on either side of the valley, and along the bottom of it there flowed a great brown river.

It's amazing that the room seems like the outdoors!

CRITICAL READING SKILL

Encourage students to include sketches of scenes in the Response Notes. This will help them "see" and remember details from the story. Ask students to highlight descriptive words with a highlighter pen.

Example:

(*suck-suck-sucking sound of the pipes*)

REREADING

Ask students to read the selection again. This time, have students mark some descriptive language in each paragraph of the selection.

Writing

In this lesson, students write a descriptive paragraph of Mr. Wonka's popcorn room.

SKETCH A PICTURE

In this activity, students pick their favorite descriptions from the story. They write them and then sketch pictures of them, using the frames on the pages. For example: *"And just look at my pipes! They suck up the chocolate and carry it away to all the other rooms in the factory where it is needed."*

Ask students what they liked about this description. Have them write their rationales. For example, *"It's so easy to imagine how the chocolate moves through the pipes to other rooms."*

Sample Response: →

THE POPCORN ROOM

In this activity, students use descriptive words and details to write one paragraph descriptions of Mr. Wonka's popcorn room. Encourage students to use word webs to brainstorm images and details they might include.

Sample Response

The first thing I noticed was the pop-pop-popping sound. It was anything but relaxing. Little puffs would fly up into the air. I felt like I was walking into a room full of packing material. We had to put on white overalls, so we all looked like giant, oversized pieces of popcorn. I started jumping.

WRITING REMINDERS

As students plan their descriptive paragraphs, remind them to:

✔ Outline the points they want to make.

✔ Use at least three descriptive words.

✔ Use details to help create vivid pictures in readers' minds.

For use with page 71

Unit Overview

In this unit, students learn to compare and contrast, identify cause and effect, and follow a sequence of events in order to get more out of what they're reading. Explain that asking how things are alike and different is one way to think about a topic as they're reading. So is identifying cause and effect, which helps them understand why things happened. Keeping track of the sequence, or time order, of a story helps them picture the unfolding of an event as it happens. Tell students that when their minds are actively engaged, they can appreciate, understand, and retain more of what they read.

Reading the Art

Have students look at the artwork and read the unit introduction. Ask students:

- What is the boy doing?
- What do the bubbles represent?
- How do the graphics visually represent the three stories in this unit?
- How might these techniques (compare and contrast, cause and effect, and sequencing) come in handy as you read the selections?

Literature Focus

Lesson	Literature
1. Alike and Different	**Selby B. Beeler**, from *Throw Your Tooth on the Roof* This nonfiction selection is about what children all over the world do when they lose their baby teeth.
2. Asking Why	**Jean Fritz**, from *And Then What Happened, Paul Revere?* This is a true story about what Paul Revere did to prepare for the night of his big ride.
3. Time Order	**Jean Craighead George**, from *One Day in the Prairie* The passage describes a period of 35 minutes in the morning on an Oklahoma prairie. The events described are arranged according to the time at which they occurred.

Reading Focus

Lesson	Reading Skill
1. Alike and Different	To compare, ask yourself: How are these things alike? How are they different?
2. Asking Why	When you read about a series of events, look for causes and effects, or events that bring about other events.
3. Time Order	As you read, look for sequence words to help you keep track of the order of events.

Writing Focus

Lesson	Writing Assignment
1. Alike and Different	Interview a few classmates about what they do with their lost baby teeth, and write their responses in an interview form.
2. Asking Why	Write a journal entry describing how you would feel if you were Paul Revere and were dealing with the events of this selection.
3. Time Order	Write about how you would react to a weather emergency, being careful to keep in mind and make clear in your writing the time order and sequence of the things you would do.

Alike and Different

Before Reading

FOCUS

To compare, ask yourself: How are these things alike? How are they different?

In the lesson, students learn to recognize comparisons by identifying things that are alike and different in a piece of writing.

BUILDING BACKGROUND

Vocabulary Warm-up

To familiarize students with some of the vocabulary, complete the **Cloze Sentences** below. Write the five words below on the board. Have student volunteers read the sentences with the correct words added.

 replace   *present*   *coop*   *gazelle*   *tissue*

1. The small, graceful _____ ran swiftly through the grass.
2. To my mother, cleaning the kitchen was the best _____ I could give her.
3. I found three eggs hidden in the straw of the chicken _____.
4. If they _____ the swings, the playground will be safer.
5. She wrapped the glass bird in _____ to protect it.

Prereading Strategy

Help students prepare for this selection on traditions involving teeth by creating a **Word Web**. Write the word *tooth* on the board. Write the following questions on the arms of the web. Encourage students to add one more arm with a new question.

Why do teeth have different shapes?   (*tooth*)   *What did you do with your baby teeth?*
How do you care for your teeth?

Reading the Selection

RESPONSE STRATEGY

Students identify how the traditions in this selection are alike and how they are different. Get students started by asking them to read the first two traditions and then ask:

 Sample Response:

What is the subject? *losing your baby teeth*

How has the author organized the subject? *He includes the traditions of children in different countries related to losing their baby teeth.*

Suggest that students underline the main idea of each tradition. Remind them to check the description that is most like their own.

CRITICAL READING SKILL

If students have a difficult time naming what is alike and different, encourage them to put countries that are alike in groups (for example Cameroon, India).

REREADING

Have students reread the selection to see if they can find any more elements that are alike or different.

Writing

In this lesson, students interview three or four friends regarding their traditions when they lose a tooth and record the information in a chart that compares their answers.

WHEN I LOSE A TOOTH

In this activity, students describe what they do when they lose teeth. Some students may want to describe their traditions in paragraph form, while other students may want to make lists.

Sample Response:

1. First my mom pulls out my tooth. 2. We wash it. 3. I put it in a handkerchief pillow my grandma gave me. 4. I get to choose what to have for dinner that night. 5. I put the tooth under my pillow. Then the tooth fairy comes. She takes my tooth and gives me a shiny new quarter.

LOST TOOTH TRADITIONS

In this activity, students compare and contrast lost tooth traditions of four countries by completing the chart. Suggest that students skim the selection again and highlight the four countries they are looking for (Sweden, Spain, Afghanistan, and Bangladesh). Have them read to see what is alike and what is different about the traditions of Sweden and Spain. Then they can do the same for Afghanistan and Bangladesh.

Sample Response:

Afghanistan and Bangladesh (Alike): Kids drop their teeth in a mouse (or rat) hole and make wishes to get back a rat's tooth. (Different): In Afghanistan they hope for a mouse tooth only. In Bangladesh they hope for a mouse tooth and usually get a present instead.

Have students share their answers in a whole-class discussion.

INTERVIEW FORM

In this activity, students ask three or four classmates or friends what they do when they lose teeth. Have students identify how the answers are alike or different.

Sample Response:

Aisha: She puts her tooth in an envelope and leaves it by her bed. While she's asleep the tooth fairy comes, takes her tooth, and leaves her a dollar.

Jed: He puts his tooth under the pillow in an envelope. When he wakes up the tooth is there but there is also a dollar. Alike: Both kids put their teeth in envelopes. They both get a dollar. Different: Aisha puts her tooth by the bed and the tooth fairy takes it. Jed puts his under his pillow, but the tooth fairy leaves his tooth.

WRITING REMINDERS

As students record their interviews, remind them to:

✓ Interview at least three friends or classmates.

✓ Record each person's lost tooth tradition.

✓ Include enough details to compare and contrast answers.

2 Asking Why

B e f o r e R e a d i n g

In the lesson, students study and learn to recognize cause and effect to understand why things happen.

BUILDING BACKGROUND

1. Vocabulary Warm-up

steeple   petticoat   muffled   spurs   launched

To make sure that students understand the words in this selection, try a **Vocabulary Quiz Show.** Write each word on a 3 x 5 file card. Then write a definition for each word on five other cards. Pass out the cards to 10 different students in class. Ask one student to begin by saying one of the words. Have the student with the meaning of the word on his or her card read it aloud.

Prereading Strategy

Build more background for the selection by using an **Anticipation Guide** to help students begin to focus on the selection. Encourage students to discuss their answers.

1. Agree   Disagree   The British fought against the French in the Revolutionary War. *(Disagree. The Americans gained their independence from Britain as a result of the Revolutionary War.)*

2. Agree   Disagree   The Revolutionary War was fought on the west coast of the United States. *(Disagree. The war was fought on the east coast.)*

3. Agree   Disagree   The colonists talked to each other mainly by telegraph and telephone. *(Disagree. The telephone and telegraph weren't invented yet.*

R e a d i n g t h e S e l e c t i o n

RESPONSE STRATEGY

Students are asked to circle examples of cause and effect in the selection.

Sample Response:

He was in such a hurry that he left the door open (cause), and his dog got out (effect).

CRITICAL READING SKILL

Have students read through the entire selection once. Then ask them to reread the selection and mark places that show cause and effect. If students have difficulty in identifying examples, ask them questions about sequence.

What comes first? Did something happen as a result? *(Paul left the door open and his dog got out).*

Look for ways that things are connected. *(Two lanterns were to be hung if the English came by water, one lantern if they came by land).*

REREADING

Have students reread the selection to see if they can identify one more example of cause and effect.

L i t e r a t u r e   F o c u s

Lesson	Literature
1. Skim First	**Steve Otfinoski**, from *The Kid's Guide to Money*
	This nonfiction selection describes the types of services banks offer, the advantages of storing your money there, and the process kids have to go through to use a bank.
2. Tell It Like It Is	**Stephen Kramer**, from *Avalanche*
	This selection is about the dangerous power of an avalanche and the way that avalanche rescue teams operate to try to save people trapped under the snow.
3. Using Graphic Aids	"Settling the Midwest"
	The selection focuses on the different groups who lived in the Midwest at different times, and about conflict over rights to the territory. It is supplemented with many maps and graphic aids.

R e a d i n g   F o c u s

Lesson	Reading Skill
1. Skim First	Skimming and scanning before you read can help you learn what the selection is about.
2. Tell It Like It Is	When you summarize a story or article, you tell only the most important ideas.
3. Using Graphic Aids	Graphic aids help you understand what you read and keep track of what you've learned.

W r i t i n g   F o c u s

Lesson	Writing Assignment
1. Skim First	Create a poster that would help younger students understand the process of skimming and scanning.
2. Tell It Like It Is	Write a paragraph summarizing the selection.
3. Using Graphic Aids	Fill in the chart provided in order to organize the information from the selection.

1 Skim First

Before Reading

FOCUS
Skimming and scanning before you read can help you learn what the selection is about.

In the lesson, students learn how to skim an article to find out what it's about.

BUILDING BACKGROUND

Vocabulary Warm-up

Prepare for the lesson with this **Context Clues** activity. Write these vocabulary words and the sentences that follow on the board. Ask students to define each word, using clues within the sentences to help them.

deposit   interest   investment   guardian   designated

1. The couple regularly <u>deposit</u> money in their account; they put $10.00 in their savings account each Monday. *(Put is a synonym for deposit.)*
2. He was pleased to see that he had earned an extra $5.00 in <u>interest</u> for keeping a savings account. *(From the sentence, it is clear that interest is money that grows when it is kept in the bank.)*
3. Buying a house was a good <u>investment</u>; they could sell it and probably make some money when they moved. *(An investment is a sum of money that is spent with the intent of gaining a profit.)*
4. When she traveled to France, her <u>guardian</u> assumed all the responsibilities of her parents. *(Guardian is a synonym for custodian or parent substitute.)*
5. The water mark on the wall <u>designated</u> the flood's high points; it showed where the water reached. *(Showed is a synonym for designated.)*

Prereading Strategy

Build more background for the selection with this **Previewing** activity. Ask students to skim the first page of the selection quickly and then answer these questions.
1. What is this article trying to convince you to do? *(save money)*
2. What is a bank good for? *(keeping money safe)*
3. What do you do with money that you don't want to spend? *(piggy bank, shoe box)*

Reading the Selection

RESPONSE STRATEGY

Students are asked to skim the selection. As they skim they are to keep track of the reasons kids should put money in the bank in the Response Notes.

Sample Response:

Banks are safe, earn interest, and help you save money instead of spending it.

CRITICAL READING SKILL

Have students begin by skimming the article. Ask students questions about the article.

Sample Response:

What clues does the article give you about the subject and content? *(title, bold headings, numbered list)*

Why do you think skimming is a skill good readers use? *(It helps them predict what the article is about, which helps them focus on and remember more of the content.)*

REREADING

Remind students that skimming doesn't take the place of reading thoroughly. They should also go back and read carefully to pick up more details.

Writing

QUICK ASSESS

Do students' posters:

✓ include at least three tips for skimming and scanning?

✓ present the information in an interesting way for younger students?

✓ show creativity?

In this lesson, students create a poster of tips about skimming and scanning.

SAVINGS EXPERIENCE

In this activity, students describe their experiences with saving money.

Sample Response:

To be honest, I never saved money until this year. It sat on my dresser and looked at me until I spent it. But on my birthday, my dad helped me open a savings account. Now I have over $75.00 in it! I really like getting the interest!

ORGANIZER CHART

In this activity, students complete organizer charts to show what they learned about banks. Encourage students to scan the article to find the answer to each question. Suggest that they use the headings and numbered list items for hints on where the answers to each question might be found.

Sample Response:

Four reasons to put your money in a bank: 1. Banks are safe. 2. Money earns interest. 3. Banks have other helpful services. 4. Banks help you save your money.

TIPS FOR SKIMMING AND SCANNING

In this activity, students share the information they learned on skimming and scanning with younger students. Explain to students that when they know something well, they can explain it in their own words. Ask them to consider their audience. How can they make the information interesting and relevant to them? Will they organize the information differently for a younger audience? Encourage them to review their Response Notes to help them decide what information to include on their posters. Some students may want to add graphics.

Sample Response:

Tips To Make You a Smart Reader 1. Be Smart...Read the title. 2. Be Smart...Look at chapter titles or bold headings. 3. Be Smart . . . Look at all the pictures and graphs. 4. Be Smart...Look at each paragraph. That's the way to skim and scan.

WRITING REMINDERS

As students complete their posters, remind them to:

✓ Include at least three suggestions in their own words.

✓ Double-check to make sure they have spelled each word correctly.

✓ Be creative in making the information interesting for younger kids.

2 Tell It Like It Is

Before Reading

FOCUS

When you summarize a story or article, you tell only the most important ideas.

In the lesson, students learn to summarize the most important ideas in a piece of writing.

BUILDING BACKGROUND

Vocabulary Warm-up

probe avalanche expert curled goggles

Be sure students understand the words above. A **Vocabulary Quiz Show** will help students learn these words in the story. Write each word on a 3 x 5 file card. Then write a definition for each word on five other cards. Pass out the cards to ten students in class. Ask one student holding a word card to say the word, and have the student holding the card with the meaning of the word read it aloud.

Prereading Strategy

Use this **Think-Pair-and-Share** activity to help students predict what they will learn. Divide the class into pairs. Ask students to read these sentences and then discuss the questions that follow:

1. "People buried by an avalanche usually cannot move their arms or legs—even if they are covered by only one or two feet of snow."
2. "Speed is important in all rescue work."
3. "They look for a glove, hat, ski tip, or any other sign that the buried person is near the surface of the snow."
4. "The rescuers hope a probe will touch the buried person so they will know where to dig."

What do you think you'll learn about in this selection? *(something about being buried in snow)*

What are the dangers of skiing? *(getting caught in an avalanche)*

Reading the Selection

RESPONSE STRATEGY

Students are asked to highlight the most important ideas with a highlighter.
Sample Response:

Everyone who spends time in snowy mountains needs to watch out for avalanches.

CRITICAL READING SKILL

Encourage students to read the entire article and then make a list of the main ideas. Tell students that sometimes a new paragraph signals a new idea.
Remind students that sometimes several paragraphs can expand on the same idea (speed is important in rescue work). For example, several paragraphs describe *how* rescuers attempt to quickly locate a person buried in an avalanche. These ideas can also be considered main ideas.

REREADING

Have students reread the selection once more and think carefully about the main ideas. If they have trouble, suggest that students ask themselves, What is the subject of the paragraph? What is the author saying about the subject?

W r i t i n g

In this lesson, students write one-paragraph summaries in their own words.

AVALANCHE NOTES

In this activity, students use the chart to take notes on each page of the selection. Tell students to look back over their highlighted text and Response Notes to see how they would break up the selection into three main ideas each for pages one and two. If students identified more (or fewer) ideas than three, suggest that they see if ideas can be combined or expanded. Remind them to write the main ideas in their own words.

Sample Response:

(Page 1) 1. There are a lot of avalanches. 2. People need to be careful and watch out for avalanches. 3. People who survive can describe what happened.

(Page 2) 1. People buried in an avalanche usually can't move. 2. Speed is important in rescues. 3. They look for a hat, gloves, or clothes. 4. A probe is used sometimes.

Have students discuss their answers as a whole class. Mention that students will have slightly different ideas. There can be more than one correct answer.

AVALANCHE SUMMARY

In this activity, students write one-paragraph summaries of the selection. Explain that they can use their notes and the previous activity to help them. Remind students that summaries are always to be written in their own words. A one-paragraph summary may have some added information but will not include the detail of the original selection.

Sample Response:

A lot of avalanches happen every year. People need to know what to do and how to be safe. One person who survived remembers being moved along downhill by the snow. He was lucky because he wasn't buried. When people are buried they are hard to find. Rescuers have to find them quickly. They make a quick search and look for signs of clothing or equipment. They also use avalanche probes. They poke the probes down into the snow to try to find the buried person.

WRITING REMINDERS

As students complete their summaries, remind them to:

✔ Include the main ideas from the selection.

✔ Write in their own words.

✔ Indent their paragraphs.

3 Using Graphic Aids

B e f o r e   R e a d i n g

FOCUS
Graphic aids help you understand what you read and keep track of what you've learned.

In the lesson, students learn to get information from graphic aids.

BUILDING BACKGROUND

Vocabulary Warm-up

Make sure students are familiar with these five words by completing the **Cloze Sentences** that follow. Write the five words and sentences on the board. Have students read the sentences with the correct word added. Then, let students make up new sentences for each word.

> *defeated   issues   conflicts   settlers   challenges*

The new arrivals were _____ who had come from the East.

The teacher helped her students resolve their own _____.

She enjoyed the _____ of learning Spanish by living with a family in Spain.

Although they didn't win, the _____ team played well.

Most of the _____ of the school election were about the cafeteria rules.

Prereading Strategy

In this selection, students learn about pioneers. Help them to build background for reading by creating a **Word Web**. Write the word *pioneer* on the board in a circle. Then write these questions on arms of the web:

Why do some people today leave their homes and move to a new country?

What caused settlers to leave their homeland?

Where would you go to be a pioneer in the 21st century?

pioneer

What hardships did they encounter in their travels?

R e a d i n g   t h e   S e l e c t i o n

RESPONSE STRATEGY

Students are asked to circle names, dates, and places as they read the selection and write down the information gleaned from the map.

Sample Response:

(circled): 1600s, Midwest, France, French trappers, Great Lakes, British trappers; (learned from map): some Midwest states, how settlers came, rivers, when they moved

CRITICAL READING SKILL

Encourage students to use the circled information to draw conclusions. For example, students may conclude that St. Louis was a major Midwest city at that time because of its location on the steamboat line. Then they can see whether information in the text supports their conclusions.

REREADING

Have students read the selection once more. Encourage them to recheck the map to see if they can add any additional notes. These questions may help:

What new information do you gain from the map on page 95? (*It shows the beginning of the steamboat line for one family who eventually got to St. Louis and then to Princeton. It also shows land and water routes.*)

Why are maps a good source of information? (*They pack a lot of information into a small space.*)

Writing

In this lesson, students complete a chart that helps them keep track of what they read.

USING THE MAPS

In this activity, students use the maps to find specific information. The circling will help them locate information easily. Answer all the questions on the page. Supply questions first, then answer.

1. How many wagons did the Culbertsons use to travel west?

(Two)

2. What mountains did the Culbertsons cross?

(The Appalachian Mountains)

3. What states did they travel along or pass through?

(Pennsylvania, Ohio, Virginia, Kentucky, Indiana, Illinois, Missouri, Iowa)

4. How did the Culbertsons travel—on land, on water, or both?

(On both: They traveled on land in a wagon and on water on ferries)

5. On what rivers did they travel?

(On the Ohio River and the Mississippi River)

6. Where did the Culbertsons build their new home?

(In Princeton, Iowa)

ORGANIZATION CHART

In this activity, students locate information from the passage to complete the chart. Remind them to observe which pieces of information are missing from the three columns. The dates, which they circled, will help them to locate the information in the text.

Sample Response:

	Did what?	**Where?**
1840s–1850s:	headed farther west	to Oregon and California

WRITING REMINDERS

As students complete their charts, remind them to:

✓ Use their circling to help them locate specific information in the text.

✓ Use the maps as well as text to find information.

✓ Complete the entries in their own words.

U n i t   O v e r v i e w

In this unit, students learn to appreciate the power of words and language. Simply by a choice of words, an author may have very different effects on the reader. In using personification, the author chooses to tell a story through the eyes—and words—of an animal, idea, or object. Or, an author may use onomatopoeia, selecting words that help the reader "hear" what the author is saying. Through these techniques, the language of an author is enlivened and compelling images are created. Active readers identify these techniques and explore the relationship to the writing.

R e a d i n g   t h e   A r t

Have students look at the artwork. What images are represented? Ask students:

- If the artwork were a book illustration, how might the author use personification?
- How is onomatopoeia used in this illustration?
- What if the illustration were used for a children's book? What words might you choose to describe the images, and why?
- Instead, what if the artwork were from a very scary movie? What words might you choose to describe the images now?

UNDERSTANDING LANGUAGE

Literature Focus

Lesson	Literature
1. The Power of Words	**Sid Fleischman,** from *The Whipping Boy* This selection is about a spoiled prince and his whipping boy, a commoner who is beaten when the prince does something wrong because it is forbidden to punish a prince. The whipping boy refuses to show emotion like the prince wants him to, and wants to go back to his normal life.
2. Is It Human?	**James Howe,** from *Bunnicula* This is a story told by a dog about his life and then about a mysterious bundle that his family brings home with them.
3. Onomato—*what?*	**Eve Merriam,** "Weather" This is a poem about rainy weather that uses many words that sound like what they mean.

Reading Focus

Lesson	Reading Skill
1. The Power of Words	Sometimes the best part of a story or poem is the words the writer uses.
2. Is It Human?	Personification is when a writer gives an idea, object, or animal human qualities.
3. Onomato—*what?*	Writers use onomatopoeia to engage the reader's "sense of sound."

Writing Focus

Lesson	Writing Assignment
1. The Power of Words	Rewrite part of the selection, replacing some of Fleischman's original words with your own and comparing the two versions.
2. Is It Human?	Write a diary entry from the perspective of and using the voice of a pet.
3. Onomato—*what?*	Write a poem about a summer rainstorm that includes onomatopoeia.

The Power of Words

B e f o r e *R e a d i n g*

FOCUS

Sometimes the best part of a story or poem is the words the writer uses.

In the lesson, students learn to appreciate authors' word choices and how those words make them feel.

BUILDING BACKGROUND

Vocabulary Warm-up

To help students learn words from this selection, use this **Matching Definitions** activity. Write the five words below and their definitions in two columns on the board. Ask students to match them by drawing a line between the word in the left column and the definition in the right column. Have students use each word in a sentence.

1. *defiantly*   feeling regret or shame for an act or shortcoming
2. *humble*   boldly resisting
3. *exasperation*   modest, meek, mild
4. *contrite*   howl
5. *yowl*   irritation or annoyance

Prereading Strategy

Give students more introduction to the selection with this **Previewing** activity. To begin, ask students to skim the first four paragraphs of the story. Then ask them to answer these four questions, based on a quick first reading.

1. What words would you use to describe the prince? *(sneaky, naughty, tricky)*
2. What type of story (genre) do you think this is? *(fairy tale, humorous story)*
3. What do you think will happen next? *(People will get irritated with the prince.)*
4. How does this prince act compared to princes in other stories you've read? *(The prince is usually brave and obedient in fairy tales. He doesn't cause trouble!)*

R e a d i n g *t h e* *S e l e c t i o n*

RESPONSE STRATEGY

Students are asked to note their responses to language in the Response Notes.

   Sample Response:

The young prince was known here and there (and just about everywhere else) as Prince Brat. ☺

CRITICAL READING SKILL

Talk to students about how skillful writers weave words that have many different effects on people. Give students the chance to brainstorm some of these responses. It will be easy for students to identify places that make them laugh. Challenge them to find at least one example that:

➤ surprises them
➤ confuses them
➤ makes them smile

REREADING

Have students read the selection once more. Ask them to add comments about some places they marked in the Response Notes.

Writing

In this lesson, students rewrite a part of the selection.

THE PRINCE AND THE WHIPPING BOY

In this activity, students describe how they feel about the prince and the whipping boy. Ask students to back up their answers with specific references from the text.

Sample Response:

Prince: I think the prince was very mean to let the whipping boy get punished. He was awful when he said it wasn't fun if the whipping boy didn't bawl. The prince was funny at times, but I wouldn't want him to be my friend. Whipping boy: He was brave. I was glad that he escaped at the end.

A CLOSER LOOK

In this activity, students write a synonym for each "colorful" word listed. Tell students that authors choose their words very carefully. Ask them to pick their favorite words and tell why they're better choices than the synonyms they found for them.

Sample Response:

Bawl; synonym, cry. Bawl just makes me see the person's face all wrinkled up and red! Cry is a boring word.

REWRITE *THE WHIPPING BOY*

In this activity, students rewrite a short section of *The Whipping Boy* by replacing all the underlined words with words of their own. Remind students to replace additional words if desired. Do their versions have the same effect? Why or why not? Some students may want to finish the story, just for fun.

Sample Response:

In the tower chamber, the prince <u>looked at</u> him with a <u>mean-looking face</u>....

Remind students to make sure the synonyms fit into the sentence correctly. For example, replacing *yowl* with the word *crying* would not fit into the sentence. Students would have to use the word *cry*.

WRITING REMINDERS

As students complete their rewrites, remind them to:

✓ Replace all underlined words with words of their own.

✓ Choose words that are synonyms.

✓ Be creative.

 **Is It Human?**

B e f o r e R e a d i n g

FOCUS

Personification is when a writer gives an idea, object, or animal human qualities.

In the lesson, students learn how giving an animal, object, or idea human qualities can make a story more interesting to read.

BUILDING BACKGROUND

Vocabulary Warm-up

Use this **Context Clues** activity to introduce the vocabulary for this lesson. Write the following five words and sentences on the board. Ask students to define each word, using clues to help them.

admonition   radiator   digress   reverie   glistening

1. The noisy <u>radiator</u> quickly heated the room. *(The function of a radiator to heat is clear from the sentence.)*
2. My parents gave me a new computer with the <u>admonition</u> to finish my schoolwork before I played any games. Though good advice, their warning was hard to follow! *(The words* warning *and* advice *explain the meaning of* admonition.*)*
3. I found myself daydreaming about a small cabin by a lake; it was a peaceful <u>reverie</u>. *(Daydreaming* provides a synonym for *reverie.)*
4. The delicate spider web <u>glistened</u> with dew, sparkling as it caught the morning light. *(The description and* sparkling *help the reader understand what* glistened *means.)*
5. Whatever the topic is, my mind wanders, and I <u>digress</u> to talk about my puppy. *(Changing the topic to talk about the puppy helps to understand the meaning.)*

Prereading Strategy

Use this **Think-Pair-and-Share** activity to prepare students to read this selection.
1. "I shall never forget the first time I laid these now tired old eyes on our visitor."
2. "That's something they always say to me when they go out: 'Take care of the house, Harold.'"
3. "...I'd rather be stretched out on my favorite rug in front of a nice, whistling radiator."

➤ Who is telling the story? *(Harold)*
➤ How would you describe the kind of life Harold and Chester prefer? *(quiet, comfortable, relaxed)*
➤ What do you think will happen next? *(I think the animals will have an adventure.)*
➤ How does the author get your attention and make you interested in the characters and plot? *(It's fun, because it's written from an animal's point of view.)*

R e a d i n g t h e S e l e c t i o n

RESPONSE STRATEGY

Students indicate parts of the story where the animals act, feel, or think like people.

Sample Response:

And people think you're being impolite if you fall asleep and start to snore, or scratch yourself in public.

CRITICAL READING SKILL

To help students identify examples of each, suggest that they write T, F, or A in the Response Notes. Encourage students to find at least three examples of each one.

REREADING

Have students read the selection once more. What question are they left with?

W r i t i n g

QUICK ASSESS

Do students' diary entries:

✓ tell the story in first-person voice from the animals' points of view?

✓ describe the events selected?

✓ show creativity?

In this lesson, students write an entry from their pet's diary.

HAROLD'S HUMAN WAYS

In this activity, students note the ways that Harold thinks, feels, and acts like a human. Have students review their circling or underlining and Response Notes to complete some of the items. Suggest that students skim the selection to find the answers to specific questions. They do not need to complete the items in complete sentences.

Sample Response:

Harold's family is: the Monroes

INVENT A PET

In this activity, students create pets that can think, act, and feel like people. Encourage students to take some time to choose their pets, although some students may want to use their real-life pets. Encourage them to be creative in their answers.

Sample Response:

Something my pet likes: pepperoni pizza with extra cheese, musicals, dancing the Salsa

DIARY ENTRY PLANNING

In this activity, students circle events to write about. Remind them that they can also choose events that are not on the list. Tell them that choosing the events will help them to create diary entries around things of interest. Once they have chosen the events, students may want to revise their notes in Activity 2 so that they better fit those events. For example, "pepperoni pizza" might be changed to "birthday cake" to better fit an occasion for a bully's visit.

Sample Response:

a bully comes over for a visit

DIARY ENTRY

In this activity, students use their notes in Activity 2 and the events chosen in Activity 3 to write entries about the events from their animals' point of view. Remind students to get inside the heads of their animals.

➢ What does the animal think about the event?

➢ How does the animal feel about what might happen?

➢ What will the animal do?

Sample Response:

I shall never forget the day Anna brought home a cat. As a dog, I hate cats. She wanted me to like that yellow, furry thing. "No way," I said, and growled. Soon she got the message, and the cat was gone.

WRITING REMINDERS

As students complete their diary entries, remind them to:

✓ Write from the animals' points of view.

✓ Keep the animals' characteristics and the events in mind.

✓ Be creative.

3 Onomato—*what?*

B e f o r e | *R e a d i n g*

FOCUS
Writers use onomatopoeia to engage the reader's "sense of sound."

In the lesson, students learn how onomatopoeia helps the reader hear what the author is saying.

BUILDING BACKGROUND

Vocabulary Warm-up
A **Vocabulary Quiz Show** will help students become familiar with these words.

slather   galosh   rumble   slither   clatter

Write each word on a 3x5 file card. Then write a definition for each word on five other cards. Ask one student holding a word card to say the word, and have the student holding the card with the meaning of the word to read it aloud.

Prereading Strategy
Help prepare students for the selection by creating a **Word Web**. Have students choose a weather word, such as *snow, rain, hurricane, tornado,* or *sunshine,* and write that word in the center of a circle. Write these questions on arms of the web:

What sounds do you hear when you are outside in this weather?

Where is the weather condition most likely to occur?

What words describe the weather?

How would you protect yourself in this kind of weather?

What activities do people do in this weather?

R e a d i n g   t h e   S e l e c t i o n

RESPONSE STRATEGY
Students are asked to underline examples of onomatopoeia and to circle any words they don't understand, noting them in the Response Notes.

Sample Response:

slosh a galosh slosh a galosh; Circled: bumbershoot

CRITICAL READING SKILL
If students have trouble recognizing examples of onomatopoeia, suggest that they read the poem softly and slowly out loud to themselves. This will help them to hear the sounds.

What does the sound seem to reflect? *(raindrops, walking through puddles)*

What does the repetition do? *(helps the reader to hear the rhythm of the sound, like raindrops hitting the window)*

REREADING
Have students reread the poem one more time and then ask them questions.

What kind of weather is it describing? *(rainstorm)*

What sounds are included in this poem titled "Weather"? *(slosh, slither, spack a spack speck, dot a dot dot)*

What does each sound represent? *(raindrops, wet cat, thunder)*

W r i t i n g

In this lesson, students write a poem about a summer rainstorm.

HAPPY OR SAD?

In this activity, students state whether the poem's narrator is happy or sad. Ask students to think about the sounds Merriam uses. Do they present a happy or a sad view of rain?

Sample Response:

I think she is happy, because the sounds are happy sounds. For example, "Puddmuddle jump in and slide!" sounds like a lot of fun!

IMAGINE A SUMMER RAINSTORM

In this activity, students think of onomatopoeia for four sounds that might accompany a summer rainstorm. Encourage students to record several ideas for each of the four sounds.

Sample Response:

The sound the rain makes: split, splat, pitypitypity

POEM ABOUT A SUMMER RAINSTORM

In this activity, students write poems about a summer rainstorm that use onomatopoeia. Remind students to use the words from their organizers in their poems. Some students may want to research storms and look at photographs of summer storms in different environments for inspiration.

Sample Response:

The rain went splish, pitter patter splish.
So I let it collect in a dish.
Then the rain came plop, plop, plop,
In very big drops.
Then the skies went crash, rumble, bang!
That's thunder and lightening, gang.

WRITING REMINDERS

As students complete their poems, remind them to:

✓ Include several examples of onomatopoeia.

✓ Use some examples brainstormed in their organizers.

✓ Be creative.

Unit Overview

In this unit, students learn about realistic fiction. They learn to identify characters that seem like people in their own lives and to make predictions about what those characters might say or do. They learn to ask "Would I have said or done that?" and to practice connecting details about the characters and experiences in books to their own lives. Tell students that visualizing themselves or people they know in a piece of writing is an active reading technique. It helps them to pay attention to the writing and get more out of their reading.

Reading the Art

Have students look at the artwork and read the unit introduction. How does the illustration provide a good introduction for this unit? Ask students:

- How does the caption tell you who the two boys are?
- Take a good look at the illustration. What makes this look like realistic fiction?
- Imagine that one boy is a character in a book you have written. What similarities might the boy who's the reader and the book character share? What might be different?
- What one detail about the character could you relate to in your own life?

READING AUTHORS

Literature Focus

Lesson	Literature
1. That Could Be Me!	**Judy Blume**, from *Otherwise Known as Sheila the Great*
	This is a piece of realistic and humorous fiction about a girl named Sheila who is nervous about getting swimming lessons and tries to get out of it, first with her mom and then with her instructor, Marty.
2. Thinking about Character	**Judy Blume**, from *Tales of a Fourth Grade Nothing*
	This is a story about Peter Hatcher, who says he has a lot of problems, the biggest of which is his younger brother Fudge. Peter wins a turtle at his friend's birthday party, and he is worried about Fudge hurting the turtle.
3. Making Connections	**Judy Blume**, from *Fudgemania*
	This is a story about how Peter and Fudge get along, which helps us learn about and feel connections with the characters.

Reading Focus

Lesson	Reading Skill
1. That Could Be Me!	As you read, try to compare yourself to a character and imagine yourself in the same situation.
2. Thinking about Character	Pay attention to a story's characters. Think about how they act and how they feel about themselves and others.
3. Making Connections	When you read, try to make a connection between the story and your own life.

Writing Focus

Lesson	Writing Assignment
1. That Could Be Me!	Draw a word picture of yourself and compare it with a word picture of Sheila in order to see what the two of you have in common.
2. Thinking about Character	Write a one-paragraph description of Peter that includes a topic sentence and supporting details from the story.
3. Making Connections	Write a narrative paragraph about your most embarrassing moment, including the important details and the facts of the situation.

That Could Be Me!

Before *Reading*

FOCUS

As you read, try to compare yourself to a character and imagine yourself in the same situation.

In the lesson, students learn to compare themselves with a character who might have much in common with themselves.

BUILDING BACKGROUND

Vocabulary Warm-up

Help students become familiar with these words from the lesson with this **Matching Definitions** activity. Write the words and definitions in two columns on the board. Ask students to match each word in the left column with its definition in the right column.

1. *stomachache*   a disease of the lungs
2. *allergy*   easy; done with no difficulty
3. *nervous*   reaction of sneezing, itchy eyes, or skin rashes
4. *a cinch*   pain in the stomach area
5. *pneumonia*   tense; fidgety

Prereading Strategy

Build background for this selection by creating a **Word Web.** Write the word *swimming* on the board with a circle around it. Then write the following questions on the arms of the web. Encourage students to add one more question.

Where might a person learn to swim?   (swimming)   What was it like for you to learn to swim?

What is difficult about learning to swim?   What is it like to learn something new?

Reading *the* *Selection*

RESPONSE STRATEGY

In this lesson, students make predictions about Sheila in the Response Notes.

Sample Response:

when Marty says, "It's a cinch" to blow bubbles: I think Sheila will not want to blow bubbles. Marty will have to trick her or something.

CRITICAL READING SKILL

If students have trouble making predictions, have them stop and ask themselves: What will happen next? or What will Sheila do next? Point out the example in the Response Notes. Ask students if they agree or disagree with that prediction.

REREADING

Have students reread the excerpt one more time and think about Sheila's character.

➤ What makes Sheila such a familiar character? (*Most kids her age have had the experience of learning something new that frightened them.*)

➤ What techniques does Blume use to make her character believable? (*real dialogue; humor; Sheila is an honest character*)

➤ What kinds of excuses does Sheila use? (*stomachache, sore throat, no bathing cap, doesn't feel well, might get pneumonia*)

W r i t i n g

QUICK ASSESS

Do students' word pictures:

✓ include words that represent characteristics?

✓ use examples from their organizers?

✓ represent stick figures of humans?

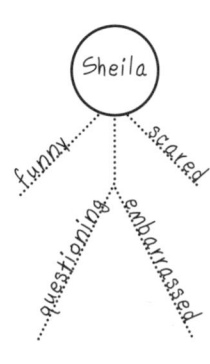

In this lesson, students draw a word picture of themselves.

SHEILA

In this activity, students describe their opinion of Sheila. Explain to students that they will have very different opinions of her. Brainstorm with the class what some of these opinions might be:

Sample Response:

too afraid, honest, funny, silly

honest

funny

silly

Remind students to back up their opinions with facts. For example, *"I think she is honest because she tells her mom and Marty that she is afraid."*

WORD PICTURE OF SHEILA

In this activity, students create a word picture of Sheila. Explain that it is another kind of word web. Have students review the selection as they jot down characteristics of Sheila in the Response Notes. Encourage students to think about where they will write each characteristic in her stick figure.

Some picture words might include: *funny, scared, questioning, embarrassed*

WORD PICTURE OF YOURSELF

In this activity, students create a word picture of themselves. First, have them make a list of their characteristics, and then place them into their word pictures of themselves. Then ask them to review the words in their word pictures of Sheila and draw a circle around any that they have in common with Sheila. For example, they might be funny, also.

Sample Response:

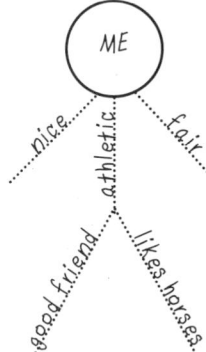

WRITING REMINDERS

As students complete their word pictures, remind them to:

✓ Think of their most important characteristics.

✓ Determine what they have in common with Sheila and what's different.

✓ Make sure their word pictures are accurate reflections of themselves.

Thinking About Character

B e f o r e   *R e a d i n g*

FOCUS

Pay attention to a story's characters. Think about how they act and how they feel about themselves and others.

In the lesson, students learn to pay attention to a character's actions and feelings toward themselves and others.

BUILDING BACKGROUND

Vocabulary Warm-up

To make sure students understand the vocabulary, have them complete these **Cloze Sentences.** Then ask them to make up sentences of their own for each word.

| angle | cushioned | groan | scrub | commercials |

1. His _____ bicycle seat made it possible to complete the cross-country bike trip.
2. There are so many _____ on television that it's hard to keep track of the story.
3. All the medical students let out a _____ when the instructor announced that they would be working night shifts in the ER starting next week.
4. They had to _____ their hands in order to get the chocolate off.
5. She tried to look at the problem from every _____ to make the best decision.

Prereading Strategy

Build background for the selection and focus students' attention by using an **Anticipation Guide.**

1. Agree   Disagree   Kids can win prizes by throwing Ping-Pong balls into little glass bowls at county fairs.
2. Agree   Disagree   In most apartment houses, it's OK to have pets like horses.
3. Agree   Disagree   Turtles cannot live in houses but have to live outside.

R e a d i n g   *t h e*   *S e l e c t i o n*

RESPONSE STRATEGY

In this selection, students are asked to underline information about Peter, the main character, and then to write what they think of him.

Sample Response:

I live at 25 West 68th Street. It's an old apartment building. But it's got one of the best elevators in New York City. About Peter: I think Peter is a neat kid. He mentions details about where he lives, and I like that. He seems happy, even though he doesn't have a yard.

CRITICAL READING SKILL

How can students figure out what to underline? Have them begin by finding the following information about Peter. They can mark where the information in text comes from with the initials M (mother), B (brother), and P (Peter).

➤ What is Peter's relationship with his mother and father? (*"She doesn't like turtles and she is always telling me to wash my hands." "He spends a lot of time watching commercials on TV."*)

➤ What is Peter's relationship with his brother? (*The only time I really like him is when he's sleeping.*)

➤ What is Peter like? (*He seems like a nice kid who thinks about stuff.*)

REREADING

Have students reread the selection to see what else they can find out about Fudge. Then ask students what they predict will happen next.

W r i t i n g

QUICK ASSESS
Do students' paragraphs have:

✓ completed topic sentences?

✓ information about the items listed in the topic sentences?

✓ examples to back up the information they include about Peter?

In this lesson, students write one-paragraph descriptions.

KNOWING SOMEONE LIKE PETER
In this activity, students write about whether they would like to know someone like Peter. Remind students to back up their writing with examples.

Sample Response:

I would like to know someone like Peter. For one thing, he doesn't pout when he doesn't get his own way, like when he ended up with a turtle instead of a goldfish like all his friends.

WHAT IS PETER LIKE?
In this activity, students complete a chart that records information about Peter. Point out to students that the chart asks not only for their answer but also for information that provides substantiation and examples. Suggest they look back at their notes. If they marked the text with M, B, and P, those notes will help. Have them underline the text that tells how Peter *acts,* how he feels about *others,* and how he feels about *himself.* Tell students that each box can have more than one answer.

Sample Response:

How does Peter act? Flexible. How Do You Know? He doesn't act disappointed when he gets a turtle instead of a goldfish like all his friends. How does he act? Good. How Do You Know? He feels bad when he won and others didn't. How does he feel about himself? He feels good about himself. How Do You Know? He thinks he can do anything. He will take care of the turtle with no problem, and he feels sorry for his younger brother, "Fudge."

DESCRIPTION OF PETER
In this activity, students write one-paragraph descriptions of Peter by first completing the topic sentence. Point out that the topic sentence has three blanks. Remind students to cover how Peter acts, how he feels about himself, and how he feels about others. Suggest that students review their notes from the previous activity, as well as their underlining of the selection, before they write. Ask them to include examples for each point they make.

Sample Response:

Peter Hatcher is a good friend. He thinks about things and doesn't just get mad, except at Fudge. Fudge makes him lose his patience. Peter has a turtle, Dribble. Dribble is important to Peter. He takes care of him and even wants to make him happy. I think that is a special thing about Peter, to want to make his turtle happy.

WRITING REMINDERS
As students complete their paragraphs, remind them to:

✓ Check to see that they have topic sentences.

✓ Make sure that the paragraphs contain information about all three items mentioned in the topic sentences.

✓ Include examples of the main points they include about Peter.

3 Making Connections

Before *Reading*

FOCUS

When you read, try to make a connection between the story and your own life.

In the lesson, students practice connecting the characters and story line to their own lives.

BUILDING BACKGROUND

Vocabulary Warm-up

pretending	fainted	clutched	moaned	overdoing

To make sure students understand these words, try a **Vocabulary Quiz Show**. Write each word on a 3x5 file card. Then write a definition for each word on five other cards. Pass out the cards to 10 different students in class. Ask one student to say one of the words, and have the student with the definition card read it aloud.

Prereading Strategy

Use this **Think-Pair-and-Share** activity to help get students ready to read.

1. "'And the Tubmans are going to be next door?' I couldn't believe this. 'Sheila Tubman . . . next door . . . for two whole weeks?'"
2. "'Sheila Tubman,' Fudge said."
3. "'And this house is right next to the place they've rented for their vacation,' she told me."
4. "'Don't say that name around me,' I told him, 'or I'll faint again.'"

➤ In what order do these sentences occur in the story? *(2, 4, 3, 1.)*
➤ How do you think Peter feels about Sheila? *(He says he'll faint. It sounds like he has a lot of problems with Sheila.)*
➤ What is taking place this summer that surprises Peter? *(His family is renting the summer house next door to a cottage rented by the Tubmans.)*

Reading the Selection

RESPONSE STRATEGY

In this selection, students relate the characters and events to things in their own lives by marking details that are similar. They also comment in the Response Notes.

Sample Response:

"'Guess what, Pete?' my brother, Fudge, said. 'I'm getting married tomorrow.'" Comments: My Dad would play along with the stuff I would say to him. If I said I was going to the moon, my dad would write down the exact address so he could send me a letter there.

CRITICAL READING SKILL

Encourage students to read the selection for enjoyment. Have them mark with a star or other symbol the details that remind them of something in their own lives, and make comments in Response Notes.

REREADING

Have students reread the selection and ask themselves, "What in the story reminds me of my own life?" Tell them to write the memories in the Response Notes.

Writing

In this lesson, students write paragraphs about their most embarrassing moments.

MY OWN LIFE

In this activity, students identify the details in the story that remind them of themselves or their own lives. Tell students that a list is fine.

Sample Response:

throwing teddy bears, going to the beach, Peter's reaction to Sheila

MY EMBARRASSING MOMENT ORGANIZER

In this activity, students complete organizer charts around their most embarrassing moments. Tell students that this is another way to organize their ideas in preparation for writing.

Sample Response:

Who was there?
I was in the back seat with grandma and Casey, our dog

Where did it happen?
while we were on vacation. . . in the car

EMBARRASSING MOMENT TOPIC SENTENCE

In this activity, students write topic sentences about their embarrassing moments. Remind students that a topic sentence tells readers what the paragraph is about. Have them read the example sentence and then write their own. Suggest that they refer to their notes from the last activity to help them.

Sample Response:

My most embarrassing moment happened two years ago when, believe it or not, I accidentally fell out of the bathtub.

MY MOST EMBARRASSING MOMENT

In this activity, students create paragraphs about their embarrassing moments, using information from their organizers and topic sentences. Tell students that their paragraphs should do more than "report" the event. Details make the event come alive for readers.

Sample Response:

It's hard to say how this happened, but two years ago I accidentally fell out of the bathtub right in front of my little sister, who was brushing her teeth at the time. It was one of those curvy, slippery-sided tubs, and as I started to slip I grabbed the towel rack that was on the wall. The towel rack came off the wall in my hand. Out I flew, bursting through the shower curtain and gracefully sliding across the floor. I came to rest with my other arm in the toilet. "Hey, what's up?" were my first words to my sister, who was just standing there, toothpaste dribbling down her chin, her eyes as big as baseballs.

WRITING REMINDERS

As students complete their paragraphs, remind them to:

✓ Check to see that they have topic sentences.

✓ Make sure the paragraphs follow the information mentioned in the topic sentences.

✓ Include details that make the events come alive for readers.

U n i t   O v e r v i e w

In this unit, students learn to practice skills that will make them better readers. In this unit, explain to students that they will practice finding the main idea, drawing conclusions, and separating facts from opinions. Tell students that these active reading skills will help them better understand a selection and keep them focused and involved as they are reading.

R e a d i n g   t h e   A r t

Have students look at the artwork and read the unit introduction. Ask them what the artwork says about this unit, and write their ideas on the board. Ask students:

- What points does the boy seem to be introducing?
- Why do you think practicing these skills is part of being a good reader?

L i t e r a t u r e   F o c u s

Lesson	Literature
1. Is It Important?	**Linda Hirschmann**, from *In a Lick of a Flick of a Tongue*
	This piece of nonfiction is about the different things people and animals can do with their tongues, and how useful and important a tongue is.
2. It's Up to You	**Gary Soto**, from *Baseball in April*
	Michael and Jesse, two brothers, try out for a Little League team. Michael does very well in the fielding tryout, but Jesse doesn't do as well or look as good. Michael encourages Jesse and tries to show him what to do.
3. Is That a Fact?	**Dorothy Hinshaw Patent**, from *Flashy, Fantastic Rain Forest Frogs*
	This is a nonfiction piece about various aspects of rain forest frogs, including what they look like, how they behave, and where they live.

R e a d i n g   F o c u s

Lesson	Reading Skill
1. Is It Important?	When you read, look for the most important idea. This is the author's main idea.
2. It's Up to You	When you draw conclusions, you think about what you know from the text and what you know from your own life.
3. Is That a Fact?	When you read nonfiction, think about which statements are facts and which are opinions.

W r i t i n g   F o c u s

Lesson	Writing Assignment
1. Is It Important?	Write an article about a topic you know something about, remembering to include a main idea and a few supporting details.
2. It's Up to You	Write your reactions to some quotations from *Baseball in April*, drawing conclusions and stating your own thoughts and feelings.
3. Is That a Fact?	Write an informational paragraph about an animal, bird, or reptile you find interesting. Include a topic sentence and facts and opinions about the topic.

Is It Important?

Before Reading

In the lesson, students identify the main idea and supporting details in a piece of writing.

BUILDING BACKGROUND

Vocabulary Warm-up

Introduce the vocabulary in this lesson with this **Matching Definitions** activity. Write the following words and definitions in two columns on the board. Ask students to match each word with its definition.

1. *tongue* — a quick, sharp motion
2. *lollipop* — a fleshy part of the mouth that helps to take in and swallow food, and, in humans, functions as a speech organ
3. *taste buds* — bitter, tart
4. *sour* — a piece of candy on a stick
5. *flick* — located in the tongue, they help create our sense of taste

Prereading Strategy

Introduce the lesson with this **Previewing** activity. Have students quickly skim the selection. Then ask:

1. What is the subject of this selection? *(tongues)*
2. Is the reading fiction or nonfiction? *(nonfiction—it tells information)*
3. What do you think is the purpose of the selection? *(to give information)*
4. What do you *hope* is included in this essay? *(a lot of information on animal tongues)*

Reading the Selection

RESPONSE STRATEGY

In this selection, students are asked to read through the article once to find out what it's about. Then they are to circle the sentence that best tells what the article is about.

Sample Response:

However a tongue is used, it is a most important tool.

CRITICAL READING SKILL

Knowing how to find the main idea in a piece of writing is an important skill. Tell students that usually the main idea comes at the beginning of the piece, as an introduction, or in the ending, when the main point of the writing is summarized. Have them read the first and last sentences again. Ask them to explain why the last sentence better states the main idea of this article. (Example: *I think the last sentence tells what the article is about, because it says the tongue is important, and the examples in the article are about important uses. The first sentence just says you use it in a lot of ways. It could be for whistling, for example, which isn't an important use and isn't what the author talks about.*)

REREADING

Have students reread the selection. What are uses for the tongue? Ask students to find at least 3 uses for the tongue as they reread.

Writing

In this lesson, students write magazine articles on topics of their own choosing.

TWO NEW THINGS

Students first write down two things they learned about the tongue from reading the article. For some students there may be more than two new things.

Sample Response:

helps you to be understood; animals use them to repair their homes

COMPLETE THE ORGANIZER

In this activity, each student completes an organizer chart. In the center is the main idea, with four details listed around it. How could some of the ideas be combined if necessary, so that all the information is included?

Sample Response:

Main Idea: The tongue as an important tool. Details: to eat, speak, taste foods, animals: hunt, clean themselves, repair homes

PLAN YOUR ARTICLE

In this activity, students plan the topics and the main ideas for their articles. Tell students that an article topic is general, and the main idea is the aspect of the topic.

Sample Response:

My topic: tropical fish

My main idea: how to keep the tropical fish alive

DETAILS TO SUPPORT YOUR MAIN IDEA

In this activity, students identify three details that support their main ideas.

Detail #1: Start by buying healthy fish that can live together.

Detail #2: Select a tank, plants, and other items that your fish will like.

Detail #3: Clean the tank and feed them the right food.

WRITING THE ARTICLE

In this activity, students write articles for a kids' magazine. Ask the whole class:

➤ For what ages of kids will their articles be written?

➤ Are the magazines for kids who know something about the topics?

➤ Why is it important to know the audience when writing?

Sample Response:

Tropical Fish

So you have always wanted to have some tropical fish? Here are things to remember about buying fish, setting up the tank, and feeding of your fish. Otherwise, you will be throwing away your money. I know. It happened to me the first time I bought some.

Begin by talking to someone at a tropical fish store.

WRITING REMINDERS

As students complete their articles, remind them to:

✔ Check to make sure their topic sentences are covered in the articles.

✔ Gear their articles to audiences of kids of certain ages.

✔ Include details that make the topics interesting for their target audience.

2 It's Up to You

Before Reading

FOCUS

When you draw conclusions, you think about what you know from the text and what you know from your own life.

In the lesson, students learn about drawing conclusions based on their reading and experiences.

BUILDING BACKGROUND

Vocabulary Warm-up

Help students understand the new words with this **Context Clues** activity. Students should figure out the meaning of each underlined word by using clues in the sentence.

> hurled   grounders   skidded   exaggerated   nonchalantly

1. He <u>hurled</u> the ball so fast that it blew the feathers off a nearby pigeon. *(That the ball blew the feathers off a pigeon gives a clue as to the speed of a hurled ball.)*
2. Those sliding <u>grounders</u> gave the shortstop a lot of problems. They kept rolling between his legs and into the outfield. *(The fact that the grounders were rolling is a clue to the meaning of the word.)*
3. The brakes squeaked, and he slid sideways for a time as he <u>skidded</u> to an abrupt stop. *(Squeaking brakes and sliding are clues to the meaning of skidded.)*
4. He <u>exaggerated</u> his size on paper until he was three times his real height. *(The statement that he was three times his real size suggests the meaning of exaggerated.)*
5. She calmly and <u>nonchalantly</u> walked up to accept the award. *(Calmly is a synonym for nonchalantly.)*

Prereading Strategy

Have students create a **Word Web** around the word *baseball.* Write the word *baseball* in a circle on the board. Then write these questions on the arms of the web:

Where is baseball played in your town?   What makes baseball such a popular sport?

What does it feel like to try out for a sport   (baseball)   Who can play baseball, and at what level?
or for a music or dance group?

Reading the Selection

RESPONSE STRATEGY

In this section, students draw conclusions about the characters.

> *Sample Response:*

It seems like Michael will get in and Jesse won't, because Jesse didn't do very well in fielding and needed his brother's coaching.

CRITICAL READING SKILL

Drawing conclusions based on what characters say and do, and on the situation, requires readers to think while they read. To draw conclusions, ask questions such as

➤ What is *really* going on?
➤ What doesn't make sense?
➤ What information am I missing?
➤ Could a surprise be in store?

REREADING

Have students reread the selection. Ask students: When are your conclusions and hunches about the story based on your own experiences? Have students write their own experiences in the Response Notes.

W r i t i n g

QUICK ASSESS
Do students' double-
entry logs:

✔ describe their own
thoughts and feelings
about each quote?

✔ tell why they think or
feel the way they do by
giving specific examples
or details?

✔ contain complete
sentences?

In this lesson, students create double-entry logs.

HERE'S WHAT I THINK

In this activity, students practice stating their own opinions by answering *Agree* or *Disagree* to six statements. Discuss with the class how their opinions on these subjects might influence their predictions or interpretations of the story they just read. Students' opinions will vary.

Sample Response:

(Brothers always help each other. – Disagree) My brother only helps me if he has to, or if my dad makes him. I think Michael is only helping Jesse because he doesn't think Jesse could ever make the team. If he does, Michael will be really mad.

CONCLUSIONS ABOUT *BASEBALL IN APRIL*

In this activity, students draw some conclusions about the selection. Ask them to read back over any conclusions they noted in the Response Notes, along with their answers to the previous activity. To draw conclusions, they use information about the characters in the story along with their own thoughts, feelings, and experiences.

Sample Response:

Quote: "Jesse said he thought he did and imitated Michael's swing until Michael said, 'Yeah, you got it.'" My Thoughts and Feelings: It seems like Jesse sort of does whatever Michael says. He looks up to him too much, in my opinion. I was like that with my sister. So what I think is that Jesse will get up to bat and will just swing his own way and hit those balls a long way. I hope that happens! It will be a cool story if it does.

WRITING REMINDERS

As students complete their double-entry logs, remind them to:
✔ Use their own thoughts and feelings as the basis for their answers.

✔ Include specific examples or details about why they think and feel the way they do.

✔ Write in complete sentences.

3 Is That a Fact?

Before Reading

FOCUS
When you read nonfiction, think about which statements are facts and which are opinions.

In the lesson, students learn to distinguish facts from opinions.

BUILDING BACKGROUND

Vocabulary Warm-up
Use this **Context Clues** activity to figure out the meaning of five words.

  fantastic   canopy   understory   tropical   shaded

1. "Flashy and <u>fantastic</u>—that's what rain forest frogs are. They aren't just green or brown like ordinary frogs." *(Students will conclude that* fantastic *is a lot like* flashy *and means the opposite of* ordinary.)

2. "At the top of the rain forest is the <u>canopy,</u> where trees spread their leaves to gather sunlight." *(Readers form a visual picture of the tops of tall trees with their leaves spread out.)*

3. "Below the canopy is the <u>understory.</u> The understory is made up of tree trunks, vines, and bushes." *(From the context it's clear that the* understory *is lower, since tree trunks, vines, and bushes are all close to the ground.)*

4. "The rain forest looks like a <u>tropical</u> garden. Plants grow everywhere, even on other plants." *(A tropical place is lush with plants.)*

5. "The forest floor is <u>shaded</u> by the plants above, so, often, little grows there." *(Students may conclude that* shaded *means blocked from sunlight.)*

Prereading Strategy
Build more background for the selection by using an **Anticipation Guide**.

1. Agree   Disagree   The rain forest is any rainy place with lots of tall trees.
2. Agree   Disagree   Frogs are pretty much alike no matter where you go.
3. Agree   Disagree   People are trying to save the rain forests.
4. Agree   Disagree   Scientists must have fun studying the rain forest.

Reading the Selection

RESPONSE STRATEGY
In this selection, students underline three opinions and highlight three facts as they keep track of their own thoughts and opinions in the Response Notes.

  Sample Response:

Fact: <u>Some are smaller than your thumb, and others are as big as kittens.</u>
Response Notes: As big as kittens! I want to see one of those!

CRITICAL READING SKILL
Help students distinguish facts and opinions by presenting these statements. Ask which ones are facts, because they could be checked or proven. *How* could they be proven? Which statements are opinions, because, although based on facts, they cannot be proven?

"It never freezes." *(Fact. Look in an almanac for temperatures.)*
"The rain forest looks like a tropical garden." *(Opinion. It might, but it seems like everyone would have a different idea of what a tropical garden looks like.)*
"They can be blue or orange." *(Fact. You could research photos of rain forest monkeys to see if there were blue or orange ones.)*

REREADING
Ask students to reread the selection. Have them find at least one new place to add another opinion of their own.

Writing

QUICK ASSESS
Do students' paragraphs:

✓ follow from their topic sentences?

✓ include both facts and opinions?

✓ begin with a capital letter and end with a period, question mark, or exclamation point?

In this lesson, students write paragraphs with facts and opinions.

WHAT SURPRISES ME MOST

In this activity, students describe what is most surprising to them about rain forest frogs. Point out that these are *opinion* statements. They personalize the writing. After students answer the question, ask them to identify the best places to add their sentences to the existing text.

Sample Response:

I can't believe that frogs can be as big as kittens! I want to see one of those.

FACT VERSUS OPINION

In this activity, students must decide whether each statement is a fact or an opinion. Divide the class into pairs. Point out that if they are not sure they can mark "not sure" and discuss it with their partners. Remind students that factual statements can be checked or proven, opinions cannot.

Sample Response:

The tropical rain forest is a very special place. Opinion. It can't be proven, because you can't research and prove what makes something "special." It is simply a feeling.

INFORMATIONAL PARAGRAPH

In this activity, students write paragraphs about an animal, bird, or reptile they find interesting. They begin by writing topic sentences.

Sample Response:

Cuckoos probably don't have many friends. Maybe that's why I like them so much.

Then they proceed to write the rest of their paragraphs.

Sample Response:

The female cuckoo is a very sneaky bird. While other birds are away, she lays her eggs in their nest! They come back and are probably very surprised to see a young cuckoo there. Also, when the cuckoo hatches, she bumps the other eggs out. The birds don't know the cuckoo isn't their baby, plus it's the only one left, so they feed it and take care of it. What I always wonder is why cuckoos do this.

Remind students to have fun. Give them time to do some research on the animal, bird, or reptile they chose. Ask them to note the number of facts and opinions they have, so it will help them keep track. Suggest that they take notes and organize their information before they begin to write their final paragraphs.

WRITING REMINDERS

As students complete their paragraphs, remind them to:

✓ Begin by writing a topic sentence.

✓ Include both facts and opinions.

✓ Make sure each sentence begins with a capital letter and ends with a period, question mark, or exclamation point.

READING POETRY

U n i t   O v e r v i e w

In this unit, students learn to understand and appreciate the language of poetry. Explain that poetry uses words to create pictures and feelings in the minds of readers. Poets use word choice and rhythm and rhyme to help focus readers' attention on specific words and ideas. As students pay attention to these elements as they read, they are practicing active reading. Active readers consider what the poet is saying and what they think and feel about the poem.

R e a d i n g   t h e   A r t

Have students look at the artwork. How does the illustration provide a good introduction for this unit? Write their ideas on the board. Ask students:

- What is the girl doing?
- How do you think she is feeling?
- How do the words on her T-shirt tell you about the ideas covered in this unit?
- What do you think she is writing poems about?
- What feelings might she communicate in her poems?

READING POETRY

Literature Focus

Lesson	Literature
1. What Does It Mean?	**James Berry**, "Isn't My Name Magical?" This is a poem about how a name is a personal, unique, special thing and can feel magical because people can say it in so many different ways depending on what they want and how they feel.
2. Word Pictures	**Song Myong-ho**, "The Friend I Met While Running from the War" This powerful and emotional poem is about a friend the speaker met while running from a war, whom the speaker was very close with but hasn't heard from lately.
3. Rhythm and Rhyme	**Eloise Greenfield**, "Things" This rhyming, rhythmic poem is about the lasting nature of creative poetry in comparison with things like candy and sandhouses.

Reading Focus

Lesson	Reading Skill
1. What Does It Mean?	Poems can bring out different feelings in readers.
2. Word Pictures	Poets use words to paint pictures in the readers' minds.
3. Rhythm and Rhyme	Read poems aloud to hear the rhythm and the rhyme.

Writing Focus

Lesson	Writing Assignment
1. What Does It Mean?	Write a short poem about how you feel about your name.
2. Word Pictures	Write a poem about somebody with whom you have shared a special experience. The poem should paint a "word picture" and portray how you were feeling.
3. Rhythm and Rhyme	Write a short poem that features rhyme and rhythm.

What Does It Mean?

Before Reading

FOCUS

Poems can bring out different feelings in readers.

In the lesson, students learn to understand poetry.

BUILDING BACKGROUND

Vocabulary Warm-up

Familiarize students with these five words by completing the **Cloze Sentences** that follow. Write the five words and sentences on the board, then have student volunteers read the sentences with the correct words added.

   individual   haunting   electricity   echoes   blurted

1. When the _____ went out, the house was completely dark until we found the candles and matches.
2. By accident, I _____ out the secret and spoiled the birthday surprise for my mom.
3. The music score of the scary movie was _____ , and it gave me the creeps.
4. Because of one _____ who disrupted the class, we all had to stay in for recess.
5. _____ from far away seem to bounce off the canyon walls.

Prereading Strategy

Build background for the poem with this **Previewing** activity. Have students quickly skim the first three stanzas of the poem to gain background information. Ask them:
1. What is the subject of this poem? *(names)*
2. Who is speaking in the poem? *(the poet)*
3. How does he feel about his name? *(He feels his name is very special.)*
4. What do you think the main message of the poem might be? *(The poem's message is that people's names in general are magic.)*

Reading the Selection

RESPONSE STRATEGY

In this selection, students circle words and phrases that tell how the poet feels about his name and star the parts that match their feelings.

Sample Response:

...my sound switches me on to answer like it was my human electricity.
✱ ✱ My name gets blurted out in class, it is terror, at a bad time, because somebody is cross. ✱ ✱

CRITICAL READING SKILL

In this lesson, students distinguish between the author's feelings and their own. Tell students to star the places where they feel the same way as the poet. Explain that the starred feelings may be based on memories or because of simple agreement. For example, "My name gets called in a whisper I am happy, because my name may have touched me with a living voice" might remind one student of the gentle way her grandmother wakes her up for school. Another student simply agrees that it would feel good to have someone softly say his or her name. The important point is that students begin to connect poems they read with their own lives.

REREADING

Ask students to reread the selection. Remind students that a poet uses words to evoke many different feelings in the reader. Ask students:
➤ What words in Berry's poem do you remember?
➤ What feelings did Berry's poem evoke in you?

Writing

In this lesson, students write a poem.

JAMES BERRY'S FEELINGS

In this activity, students describe how James Berry feels about his name. Remind students to refer to the words they circled.

Sample Response:

James Berry feels magical and proud. I think his name reminds him that he is a special person and an important part of the whole world.

HOW DO YOU FEEL?

In this activity, students brainstorm as many words as possible for what their names mean to them. Discuss with students how many people have several feelings about their names, so their responses may not be all "good" or all "bad." If students have trouble getting started, write these questions on the board:

➤ How did you get your name?

➤ Were you named after anyone in your family? Anyone else?

➤ Who pronounces your name in a special way?

➤ Do other people have your name? How does that make you feel?

➤ When do you most *like* and *not like* to hear your name?

Some students may want to think about their name associations at a certain age, perhaps as babies, toddlers, when they began school, or as fourth graders.

Sample Response:

boring, screamed, sung, trouble, special, same as my dad's, unusual

POEM ABOUT MY NAME

In this activity, students write short poems about their names. Remind students to refer back to the Brainstorm Box in the previous activity. If students find it hard to write, encourage them to brainstorm more words until they have some that make them feel something. Then it's time to write.

Sample Response:

Baby Aisha
Dreaming I hear my name
Snuggled in my blanket
Ohhhh look at little Aisha
Ooooo what a beautiful baby
My baby self smiles
And returns to sleep.

WRITING REMINDERS

As students complete their poems, remind them to:

✔ Brainstorm words until they are ready to write.

✔ Tell how they feel about their names, perhaps at a certain age.

✔ Use words that help convey their feelings.

 **Word Pictures**

B e f o r e   R e a d i n g

FOCUS

Poems use words to paint pictures in the readers' minds.

In the lesson, students learn to identify strong feelings in poetry.

BUILDING BACKGROUND

Vocabulary Warm-up

To familiarize students with the vocabulary in this lesson, use this **Matching Definitions** activity. Write the words and definitions in two columns on the board. Ask students to match each word in the left column with its definition in the right column.

1. *piggyback* an ornamental shrub
2. *cannons* insects with large transparent wings
3. *cicadas* amounts that can be put into the mouth at one time
4. *camellias* on the shoulders of
5. *mouthfuls* large guns, used in war

Prereading Strategy

Build background for the lesson with this **Think-Pair-and-Share** activity. To begin, write these lines from the poem on the board:

1. "Dearer than a hometown friend / I haven't heard from him since,..."
2. "When the cannons' roar / came over the mountain ridge...."
3. "He went away / his father carrying him piggyback,..."
4. "the friend I met while running from the war...."

Divide students into pairs to discuss these questions:

➤ What event do you think the poet describes, and how do you know? *(war, "the cannons' roar" is a clue)*
➤ What happens as a result of the fighting? *(people have to leave their homes)*
➤ Who is the poet writing about? *(a new friend she met during the fighting)*
➤ What feeling is evoked in this poem? *(sad, lonely for a friend, worried)*

R e a d i n g   t h e   S e l e c t i o n

RESPONSE STRATEGY

In this selection, students write their feelings about the poem in the Response Notes.

   Sample Response:

I felt sad about them eating strawberries together, but now she doesn't know where her friend is. It's sad to make a friend that goes away.

CRITICAL READING SKILL

In this lesson, students consider their feelings about the poem. Ask students:

➤ What is your response to the poem itself?
➤ What does it remind you of in your own life?

   Ask students to think about the places in the poem that evoked strong feelings. Have students identify if those feelings were in response to the poem itself (P), because the poem reminded them of something in their own lives (O), or both (B).

REREADING

Ask students to reread the selection and then ask: What do you think happened to her friend?

   Sample Response:

I think they just had to go to different places. I hope he didn't die. Maybe they will meet again as grown-ups.

Writing

QUICK ASSESS

Do students' poems:

✓ paint pictures of the shared experiences?

✓ tell their feelings about the experiences?

✓ use interesting words?

In this lesson, students create word pictures of people with whom they shared special experiences.

HOW DO YOU FEEL?

In this activity, students describe their feelings about the poem. Ask students to write in complete sentences, rather than just listing adjectives.

Sample Response:

The poem made me feel upset. I have a new friend who escaped a war in his country. It made me sad to think about him when I read the poem.

CREATING A PICTURE

In this activity, students draw word pictures from the poem. Tell students to close their eyes while you read the poem out loud. What images come to mind? What feelings accompany those images? Ask students to choose the one that seems the most powerful and draw it in the framed space. Brainstorm ways they might express their feelings about the image. Remind students that the goal should be on capturing the *feeling*, not on drawing perfectly.

Sample Response:

WORD PICTURE OF MY OWN

In this activity, students create word pictures of people with whom they've shared special experiences. Encourage students to begin by making word webs of the people they chose. Ask students:

➤ What was the shared experience?

➤ How did it make you feel?

Sample Response:

My Aunt Vinnie

My Aunt Vinnie is smart and knows it.

She is sassy and knows it!

We took a car trip together that was the most fun ever

It was me, age 10, and her, age 29.

First we looked at maps.

Then we packed the car and off we went, singing at the top of our lungs.

We did what we wanted, stopped at roadside markets,

Bought silly tourist things.

She made me so happy

I wish we could go again.

WRITING REMINDERS

As students complete their poems, remind them to:

✓ Create five- to ten-line poems.

✓ Use interesting words to paint word pictures of their experiences.

✓ Describe how the shared experiences made them feel.

3 Rhythm and Rhyme

Before Reading

FOCUS
Read poems aloud to hear the rhythm and rhyme.

In the lesson, students learn to hear rhythm and rhyme in poetry.

BUILDING BACKGROUND

Vocabulary Warm-up
If students need help with the vocabulary in this lesson, organize a **Vocabulary Quiz Show**.

rhythm	*candy*	*rhyme*	*shore*	*sandhouse*

Write each word on a 3x5 card. Write the definitions on five other cards, and pass the ten cards out to students in the class. Have a student with a definition card read it aloud. Then have the student with the matching word card read the word. Ask two or three students to use the word in a sentence. Continue until you are satisfied that all students know and understand these words.

Prereading Strategy
Use an **Anticipation Guide** to help students build background to the subject and the rhythm and rhyme in "Things." How do rhythm and rhyme help communicate feelings? Ask students to explain the reasons behind their answers.

1. Agree   Disagree   Everything changes.
2. Agree   Disagree   People write poems to express their feelings and ideas at a certain time, even though those feelings may change.
3. Agree   Disagree   The rhythm of a poem helps communicate the poet's feelings.
4. Agree   Disagree   Rhyming words are only used in poems for little kids.

Reading the Selection

RESPONSE STRATEGY
In this poem, students read the poem aloud to listen for the rhythm and circle the rhyming words. Have students read the poem out loud as a group.

Sample Response:
Rhyming words circled include: store/more, shore/more...floor.

CRITICAL READING SKILL
In this lesson, students connect with the rhythm and rhyme in a poem.
Ask students to explain the effect of the repeated last lines, "Ain't got it no more / Ain't got it no more." *(It emphasizes the loss of the candy and sandhouse.)*
Have several students read the poem out loud. Suggest they try to read it like a rap, a jazzy tune, and the blues.
➤ Is it possible to bring different feelings and energies to this poem? Is this okay? *(Yes, I think it's okay to feel the way you want about a poem.)*

REREADING
Ask students to reread the poem one last time.
➤ What surprise does Greenfield give readers at the end? *(The last two lines change and do not rhyme.)*
➤ What is the effect of this ending? *(It's startling because I did not expect it.)*

W r i t i n g

In this lesson, students write a poem using rhyme.

STOMPING FEET

In this activity, students explain why the poem made them want to snap their fingers or stomp their feet. If students haven't read the poem out loud, have them do it now.

Sample Response:

I think the word "ain't" made the poem fun. It reminded me of a jump-rope rhyme or a rap tune.

CHANGING RHYTHMS

In this activity, students identify the point in the poem where the rhythm changes. Have students refer to notes made as they reread the poem earlier.

Sample Response:

The last two lines change rhythm. "Still got it / Still got it" really stick out and just hang there in mid-air.

Why do you think Greenfield did that?

Greenfield probably wanted to wake everyone up to hear her message about how poems last.

PICK A TOPIC AND BRAINSTORM

In this activity, students pick topics for their own poems and brainstorm rhymes.

Sample Response:

(Topic: Spiders) gliding/sliding, weaving/leaving

WRITE A POEM

In this activity, students use their lists of rhyming words to write short poems. Remind students to include both rhythm and rhyme in their poems. Reading their poems softly out loud as they work will help them feel the rhythm of their writing.

Sample Response:

Spider Play

On my wall you are so cool
Spinning such a little jewel.
Just a maze of
gentle strings, silver swings
Do you work all day while I'm at school?
Teeny tiny threads a weaving,
promise me you're never leaving.
Gliding on such gentle strings
Sliding down your silver swings
If you leave I know that I'll be grieving.

WRITING REMINDERS

As students complete their poems, remind them to:

✓ Refer to their word webs for ideas to include in their poems.

✓ Use their lists of rhyming words in their poems.

✓ Use rhythm and rhyme to create feelings and word pictures of their topics.

U n i t   O v e r v i e w

In this unit, students learn about the importance of word choice. Explain that good readers notice the words an author chooses. They use context clues to learn the meaning of new words and look at dialogue as a way to understand characters' thoughts and feelings. Good readers also notice sensory words that jump out at them and make them feel and see the scene being described. Part of being an active reader is asking questions about why certain words were used and what clues they hold to the meaning of the selection.

R e a d i n g   t h e   A r t

Have students study the illustration. How would they describe it? How does it provide a creative introduction for this unit? Write their ideas on the board. Then ask students:

- Why do you think each letter is drawn in a different style?
- Why is each letter on a separate piece of paper?
- What words would you use to describe each lettering style?

Literature Focus

Lesson	Literature
1. Word Clues	**Janell Cannon**, from *Verdi* This fictional story focuses on a young yellow snake named Verdi and his interactions with the older, green snakes he is supposed to become like. The older snakes are lazy, boring, and rude, and he decides he doesn't want to get old and turn green like them.
2. Dialogue is More Than Talk	**Andrew Clements**, from *Frindle* In this story, Nick makes up a new word, "frindle," and makes a big show of saying it in his language arts class. His teacher, Mrs. Granger, is unhappy with his attempts to disrupt class.
3. Use Your Senses	**Shel Silverstein**, "Sarah Cynthia Sylvia Stout Would Not Take the Garbage Out" Many sensory images and poetic devices make the reader feel that they are experiencing what happens when Sarah refuses to take the garbage out.

Reading Focus

Lesson	Reading Skill
1. Word Clues	Look for clues in nearby words and sentences to help you figure out unfamiliar words.
2. Dialogue is More Than Talk	Authors use dialogue to move the story forward and to reveal who a character really is.
3. Use Your Senses	Sensory language makes the writer's world seem real.

Writing Focus

Lesson	Writing Assignment
1. Word Clues	Pick out a word from the story that you're not familiar with, construct a word web with the clues in the text about the word, and then guess what the word might mean.
2. Dialogue is More Than Talk	Write a dialogue that might take place between Nick and Mrs. Granger one week after the "frindle" episode.
3. Use Your Senses	Write a sensory poem, making sure that each line helps the reader see, hear, feel, taste, or smell what you are describing.

1   Word Clues

B e f o r e   R e a d i n g

FOCUS

Look for clues in nearby words and sentences to help you figure out unfamiliar words.

In the lesson, students look for context clues to help understand the meaning of new words.

BUILDING BACKGROUND

Vocabulary Warm-up

Get students ready for this lesson by using **Context Clues.** Ask students to define the words, using clues within the sentences to help them.

hatchlings   zigzagged   ventured   chided   rude

1. The hatchlings followed their mama with the nervousness of any newborn animals. *(Newborn animals is a synonym for hatchlings.)*
2. The driver got increasingly tired, and soon his eyes saw highway lanes go from straight lines into wavy, <u>zigzagged</u> patterns. *(Straight as an antonym for zigzagged, and wavy, a synonym, provide clues.)*
3. She was so allergic to hay that she rarely <u>ventured</u> outside when at her uncle's farm in the summer. The risk was not worth it. *(Risk gives a clue in the second sentence.)*
4. The teacher <u>chided</u> her students for not finishing their homework. After the criticism and scolding, every student turned in the next night's assignment. *(Criticism and scolding are clues as to the meaning of chided.)*
5. Why are people so <u>rude</u> as to talk during a symphony concert? *(Talking during a symphony concert is an example of rude behavior.)*

Prereading Strategy

Provide more background for the selection with a **Word Web** activity. Draw this Word Web on the board.

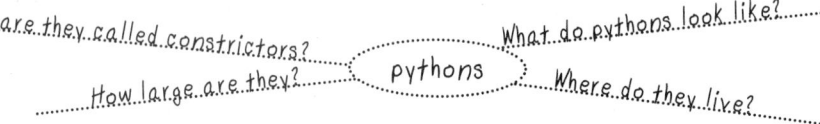

R e a d i n g   t h e   S e l e c t i o n

RESPONSE STRATEGY

In this selection, students circle words they don't know and underline ones that provide clues to their meanings.

  Sample Response:

Circled: <u>dawdled.</u> Underlined: <u>"Why the hurry...?"</u> *(In this case, "Why the hurry" helps students see that to dawdle is the opposite of "to hurry.")*

CRITICAL READING SKILL

In this selection, students practice using context clues to help them decipher the meaning of new words. To begin, have students read the selection and circle words they don't know. Next, encourage students to "think out loud" in their Response Notes as they explain which context clues help them figure out the meaning of each circled word. If students have trouble, have them work in pairs.

REREADING

Ask students to read the selection once more. Have them check to see that they have found all the context clues that help them with the words they identified. If some students seem to know all the words, have them choose three words anyway and practice identifying the context clues.

W r i t i n g

QUICK ASSESS
Do students' webs:

✔ contain the word in the center of the web?

✔ include at least two or three clues?

✔ have a definition that follows logically from the identified clues?

In this lesson, students create context clue webs.

FAVORITE WORDS

In this activity, students jot down their favorite words. Ask students on what basis a word might be a "favorite."

Sample Response:

steamy (sounds "steamy"), dawdled (I like the sound and feeling of the word as I say it), Verdi (a cute name for a baby python), lazing (it's a new word to me—it reminds me of lazy), "sporty stripes" (using the word sporty to describe Verdi's stripes makes them sound so cute. I can picture him in my mind.)

UNFAMILIAR WORDS

In this activity, students identify one to three unfamiliar words in the story and list them. If some students know all the words, have them pick any three words and list them.

A WORD WEB

In this activity, students pick one word from their lists. They refer back to the selection for clues as to the meaning, write those clues in the spaces provided, and then make a guess as to its meaning. Remind students that they may not be able to find four context clues.

Sample Response:

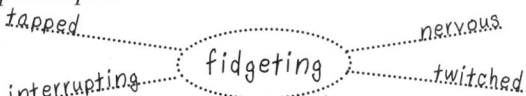

Word: fidgeting. Clues: "<u>tapped</u> a tune with his tail...," "It makes me <u>nervous</u>...," "always <u>interrupting</u>...." Meaning: I think fidgeting is when you're twitching, moving, in constant motion.

WRITING REMINDERS

As students complete their webs, remind them to:

✔ Refer back to the selection and their Response Notes.

✔ Write the clues in the spaces provided.

✔ Write the meaning of the word, based on the clues they identified.

2 Dialogue Is More Than Talk

B e f o r e   R e a d i n g

FOCUS

Authors use dialogue to move the story forward and to reveal who a character really is.

In the lesson, students look for dialogue that reveals clues about a character.

BUILDING BACKGROUND

Vocabulary Warm-up

Use this **Cloze Sentences** activity to introduce these five words before students read the selection. Write the five words and sentences on the board. Have students read the sentences with the correct words added.

launch   emphasized   disrupted   performance   maroon

1. The toy ads _____ the low cost, but failed to mention that the toy was dangerous.
2. My mom's first car was a _____ Ford. She had a purplish sweater to match!
3. The loud whir of the noisy speedboats _____ the peaceful vacation.
4. She gave her last practice _____ the week before leaving for Paris for the big concert.
5. They wanted to _____ their new software program before their rivals introduced their own.

Prereading Strategy

Build more background for this selection with this **Previewing** activity. Have students skim the first four paragraphs and then discuss these questions as a class:
1. What seems to be the subject of this selection? *(frindles)*
2. Who are the main characters? *(Nick, Mrs. Granger, John)*
3. What kind of person do you think Nick is? *(a show-off, funny, likes attention)*
4. What do you predict will happen, and why? *(maybe Nick will get in trouble or maybe a joke will be played on him. I think this because he is a show-off.)*

R e a d i n g   t h e   S e l e c t i o n

RESPONSE STRATEGY

In this selection, students underline dialogue that provides clues about Nick and Mrs. Granger.

Sample Response:

"Idea? What idea?" asked Nick, and he tried to make his eyes as blank as possible.

"You know what I mean, Nicholas. I am talking about the performance that you and John gave at the start of class."

CRITICAL READING SKILL

In this selection, students identify dialogue that helps them to learn more about Nick and Mrs. Granger. After students underline the dialogue, they can make notes in the Response Notes *"Mrs. Granger, I forgot my frindle."* (Nick is trying to get everyone's attention by using a word no one knows.)

REREADING

Ask students to read the selection once more. This time, see how the author's description of a character's body language can provide added information.

W r i t i n g

QUICK ASSESS

Do students' dialogues:

✔ build on the story?

✔ contain quotation marks around all dialogue?

✔ indent each time a new character talks?

In this lesson, students create dialogue that expands on the story.

FEELINGS ABOUT NICK

Here students explain their feelings about Nick. Suggest that their feelings may come from Nick's dialogue, from descriptions of him and his interactions with other people, and from students' own experiences with kids like Nick.

Sample Response:

I think Nick is funny, funny, funny. He reminds me of me and my friend Noah. We like to play jokes. We aren't mean, though. We just like to laugh.

NICK QUOTES

In this activity, students explain what each quote tells them about Nick. Suggest to students that they find each quote in text and highlight it. That way, they can read it in context if desired.

Sample Response:

"But I really didn't have a frindle with me," said Nick.... I think Nick was being a little bit of a smart-aleck. He isn't listening to Mrs. Granger, or at least he doesn't seem to be. He still uses the word frindle when she is saying not to disrupt the class anymore.

DIALOGUE

In this activity, students continue the conversation between Nick and Mrs. Granger one week later. Ask students these questions in preparation for their dialogues:

➤ Where does the story leave off?

➤ How do Nick and Mrs. Granger feel about each other and the frindle situation?

➤ What do you think will happen next?

Sample Response:

"No, I have managed to put my frindle in a safe place," said Nick, chuckling proudly. Two points for getting that word in a sentence in the first two minutes. John smiled at him and slapped hands.

Suddenly, Mrs. Granger's eyes flashed and then lit up—a little too brightly, thought Nick. "Nicholas," she said sweetly. "I need your help. Can you stay after school today for an hour or so?"

Nick tried to think of something important he had to do, but his mind went blank. "Uh, I guess so," he said, unable to look at her.

"Very well," said Mrs. Granger. "I'm sure I have your word on that." She smiled sweetly and then continued down the hall, humming a happy little tune. He wondered if he had pushed his word play one word too far. Time would tell.

WRITING REMINDERS

As students complete their dialogues, remind them to:

✔ Review where the story left off.

✔ Put quotation marks around all dialogue.

✔ Indent each time a new character talks.

3 Use Your Senses

Before Reading

In the lesson, students identify sensory language.

BUILDING BACKGROUND

Vocabulary Warm-up

Use this **Matching Definitions** activity to introduce new words to students. Write the words and definitions in two columns on the board. Ask students to match them by drawing a line between the word in the left column and the definition in the right column.

1. *scour*   spoiled, soured, as in milk
2. *rinds*   transparent sheet used in packaging many foods
3. *withered*   clean, scrub
4. *cellophane*   tough outer layers or peelings of fruits, for example
5. *curdled*   shriveled, shrunken from being dried out

Prereading Strategy

In this selection, students learn about garbage—and what happens when it's left a little too long. Help students prepare for the selection by creating a **Word Web.**

What happens when food is left in the refrigerator too long?

What do you think would happen if all the garbage collectors left town permanently?

garbage

Who takes out the garbage in your family?

What is the worst part about taking out the garbage?

Reading the Selection

RESPONSE STRATEGY

In this selection, students identify how Silverstein uses the senses to describe garbage.

   Sample Response:

Chunks of sour cottage cheese - smell; drippy ends of ice-cream cones - sight; It raised the roof, it broke the wall - sound; Gristly bits of beefy roasts - touch; brown bananas - taste

CRITICAL READING SKILL

In this selection, students identify which senses are involved as they read the description of the Stout family's garbage. Tell students that often more than one sense is engaged. For example, "Drippy ends of ice-cream cones" can involve a sense of touch and taste. Ask students to identify at least two descriptions that involve two senses at once. (*I can smell and taste "curdled milk." Ick. It is sickening. I can even see and hear that lumpy stuff plop-plopping out of the milk carton into the sink.*)

REREADING

Ask students to reread the poem to identify their favorite description. Ask them to help Silverstein by describing one or more new items of garbage to stack up in the Stout household. Encourage students to use interesting adjectives. (*furry green yogurt, drippy brown asparagus, dried egg yolk*)

Writing

In this lesson, students write a poem using sensory language.

DID YOU ENJOY THE POEM?

In this activity, students explain their feelings about the poem. Remind them to write in complete sentences and to use examples from the poem to back up their feelings.

Sample Response:

This is one of my favorite poems. My favorite part is when the garbage reaches from New York to California! I also like the "Chunks of sour cottage cheese" and "Gristly bits of beefy roasts." They are the most sickening of all!

WHICH SENSE?

Here students pick more favorite lines and then describe which sense, or senses, are involved. Encourage students to use their Response Notes and the descriptions circled in the poem.

Sample Response:

Rubbery blubbery macaroni – touch, taste, sight

USE YOUR OWN SENSES

In this activity, students list what they can see, hear, taste, smell, or feel now. Tell students to close their eyes in order to listen. Sometimes, blocking one or more senses helps to focus on another one.

Sample Response:

hear: lawn mower, kids on playground, pencil sharpener; smell: cafeteria lunch, rabbit cage; touch: pencil, sweater; taste: the apple I ate at recess; sight: the back of Michael's head, Mr. Brandow

SENSORY POEM

In this activity, students write sensory poems. To begin, have students think of topics for their poems. Encourage them to create word webs of ideas and images to include. If students cannot think of subjects for their poems, have them look through books or magazines for images that inspire them.

Sample Response:

Rainstorm
Puddles of water
Squish between my toes
Umbrellas turn inside out
Blasts of wind fight to turn umbrellas inside-out
I give up and drop mine in a trash can.
With dripping hair and sopping clothes, I plunge on,
Swimming my way home.

WRITING REMINDERS

As students complete their poems, remind them to:

✓ Title their poems.

✓ Make sure the descriptions fit the titles of the poems.

✓ Include at least four different sensory descriptions.

Unit Overview

In this unit, students study the writing of author Julius Lester. Explain that Lester's writing grows out of his own experiences and interests. His interest in history drew him to folktales and to writing books about the lives of slaves in America. Like most authors, Lester often communicates his message through the characters in his books. When readers connect the events or characters in his stories to their own lives, it furthers their understanding of the characters and the events. It is another way to be an active reader.

Reading the Art

Have students look at the illustration and describe the image. Ask students:

- Why do you think this image was chosen?
- Who is the woman? What is she doing?
- What is the significance of the heart? How does it change the feeling of the artwork?
- In what way could you connect what you know about this character to something in your own life?

L i t e r a t u r e   F o c u s

Lesson	Literature
1. Folktales: Part of a Tradition	**Julius Lester**, "What Is Trouble?"
	Mr. Bear says he doesn't know what trouble is, so Mr. Rabbit sets the woods around where he is sleeping on fire. Mr. Bear is very angry, but Mr. Rabbit just hops away laughing.
2. Getting to the Heart of It	**Julius Lester**, "The Knee-High Man"
	A knee-high man wants to be taller. He talks to some animals about how to get bigger, but none of their advice works. Finally, he talks to Mr. Hoot Owl, who tells him that he doesn't need to get any bigger.
3. Understanding Characters	**Julius Lester**, from *Long Journey Home*
	This story is about a group of slaves who are called in from the fields in the afternoon. The slaves are worried that there will be bad news, but they are told by their master that the South has lost the war and that they are now free.

R e a d i n g   F o c u s

Lesson	Reading Skill
1. Folktales: Part of a Tradition	Folktales entertain us and teach a lesson at the same time.
2. Getting to the Heart of It	In folktales, you can often discover the theme by looking at the lessons the characters learn.
3. Understanding Characters	Connecting to the experiences or feelings of characters helps us to understand them.

W r i t i n g   F o c u s

Lesson	Writing Assignment
1. Folktales: Part of a Tradition	Imagine that the story continues, and Mr. Bear is going to teach Mr. Rabbit a lesson. Write what lesson he would teach, and how he would do it.
2. Getting to the Heart of It	Write a short folktale that is based on a lesson you have learned in your life. Show how your character grows, changes, or learns something because of the lesson.
3. Understanding Characters	Write about a time in your life when you received important news, and how you felt about it.

1 Folktales: Part of a Tradition

Before | *Reading*

FOCUS

Folktales entertain us and teach a lesson at the same time.

In the lesson, students learn how folktales both entertain and teach a lesson.

BUILDING BACKGROUND

Vocabulary Warm-up

Help introduce new vocabulary words with a **Vocabulary Quiz Show**.

    communicating   fantasies   explanations   favor   meadow

Write each word on a 3x5 note card. Write each definition on another note card, and give the cards to ten students in class. Ask a student with a word card to read the word out loud. Help students with pronunciation if necessary. Have the student with the matching definition card read the definition out loud.

Prereading Strategy

Build students' backgrounds to this selection with an **Anticipation Guide**. What do students already know about folktales and the main characters?

1. Agree   Disagree   Bears and rabbits are natural friends. *(Disagree. Rabbits could be tasty dinners for bears.)*

2. Agree   Disagree   Bears hibernate every summer until winter. *(Disagree. Bears hibernate in the winter.)*

3. Agree   Disagree   In folktales, the weaker animal often plays a trick on or teaches the stronger animal a lesson. *(Agree. In folktales, the stronger animal sometimes is outwitted by the weaker or smaller one.)*

Reading *the* *Selection*

RESPONSE STRATEGY

In this folktale, students highlight passages that help clarify its meaning.

Sample Response:

(Highlighted) "I got so much trouble, I don't know what I'm going to do...just all kinds of trouble, Mr. Bear. What am I going to do?"

CRITICAL READING SKILL

In this folktale, students make notes in the Response Notes as they begin to understand the meaning of the story. Help students understand that stories that make a point. *(I think Mr. Rabbit really wants to get back at big Mr. Bear by tricking him. He doesn't think about how mad Mr. Bear will be though.)*

REREADING

Ask students to reread the story to find additional places that help them to understand the story. If students have trouble, ask questions about the story.

➤ What is going on? *(Mr. Bear is being very polite and nice. He doesn't think that he is being tricked by Mr. Rabbit.)*

➤ What are your feelings about what happens in the story? *(I think Mr. Rabbit is mean. (What he does is dangerous, too. But maybe he gets tired of being small and chased by big animals.)*

Writing

QUICK ASSESS

Do students' stories:

✓ include clear lessons?

✓ contain some dialogue?

✓ flow logically to the lessons that are taught?

In this lesson, students write lessons learned in a folktale.

PRETEND YOU'RE MR. BEAR

In this activity, students write from Mr. Bear's point of view. Remind students that when they write in first-person voice, they will use the pronoun "I."

Sample Response:

I feel foolish for trusting Mr. Rabbit. He tricked me. I won't try to be friends with him again. I'll just grab him and make a meal out of him.

THE MOST IMPORTANT THING

Here, students explain the message of the folktale. Tell students there is no one right answer. Have students share their ideas in a whole-class discussion.

Sample Response:

Don't be too trusting, even of someone smaller than you. They may be tricking you. Or, tricks are not a good way to teach someone.

MR. BEAR TEACHES A LESSON

In this activity, students continue the story as they tell how Mr. Bear will teach Mr. Rabbit a lesson. Ask students to begin by writing down the lesson that Mr. Bear will teach Mr. Rabbit. Then have them write their paragraphs.

Sample Response:

Lesson: It's good to respect animals that are bigger than you.

One day Mr. Bear was wandering, looking for ripe berries, when he saw Mr. Rabbit.

"Hello Mr. Rabbit," called Mr. Bear, cheerfully.

"Oh, hi Mr. Bear," said Mr. Rabbit, a bit nervously.

"Want a berry?" asked Mr. Bear.

"Sure," said Mr. Rabbit.

No sooner did he come closer than Mr. Bear grabbed him by one of his long silky ears, slung him over his back, and off they went. When Mr. Rabbit had been upside down for many hours, Mr. Bear finally set him down. He said, "Mr. Rabbit, I'm disappointed in you. I wanted to be your friend, and you tricked me. I've thought about eating you, but I don't think I want to. I want to be your friend, but if we're friends, we need to trust each other. And that would be a good choice for you, since rabbit makes a tasty dinner for a bear."

Mr. Rabbit looked at Mr. Bear, thought for about two seconds, and decided Mr. Bear was right. Maybe most rabbits and bears aren't friends, but Mr. Bear and Mr. Rabbit have been friends ever since.

WRITING REMINDERS

As students complete their stories, remind them to:

✓ Write the lesson Mr. Bear will teach Mr. Rabbit.

✓ Make sure the story teaches the lesson.

✓ Include some dialogue between Mr. Bear and Mr. Rabbit.

2 Getting to the Heart of It

B e f o r e *R e a d i n g*

In the lesson, students see how discovering what the characters learn helps them to discover the author's message.

BUILDING BACKGROUND

Vocabulary Warm-up

Use this **Cloze Sentences** activity to familiarize students with these five words. Write the five words and the sentences below on the board. Ask for students to read the sentences with the correct words added.

| stomach | bellow | throat | whip | distance |

1. The cow's loud _____ startled me out of my daydream.
2. The boxer talked big, threatening to _____ anyone who challenged him, until one day someone did and won.
3. I was so nervous that every word of my speech got stuck in my _____.
4. She had never before competed in a _____ race of over 10K.
5. If I leave my food on my plate, my mom says my eyes are bigger than my _____.

Prereading Strategy

Build more background for the story with this **Previewing** activity. Have students skim the first four paragraphs. Then discuss these questions with the whole class.
1. Who is the main character? *(the knee-high man)*
2. What is his problem? *(He wants to be taller.)*
4. What do you predict will happen, and why? *(I think he will learn something about staying the size he is, because a lot of folktales are like that.)*

R e a d i n g   t h e   S e l e c t i o n

RESPONSE STRATEGY

In this story, students record their feelings and reactions to the knee-high man.
  Sample Response:
The knee-high man takes advice that doesn't work for humans, but it's all the animals can think to tell him.

CRITICAL READING SKILL

In this story, students identify the theme by following what the main character learns.
➤ What happens to the knee-high man in the course of the story? *(He gets advice that doesn't work until he finally talks to Mr. Owl.)*
➤ What does he learn from Mr. Owl? *(He is the perfect size for him. He has no need to be as big as a horse. And when he needs to be tall, he can use his wits to help him.)*
➤ How does this become the theme? *(I think it's that we should be content with who we are and not wish that we were taller, older, bigger, or smarter.)*

REREADING

Suggest that students reread the story, to find the theme. Encourage students to ask, who is the story about? *(The knee-high man)* What does the author say about him? That's the theme. *(The theme is to be content with who you are.)*

Writing

QUICK ASSESS
Do students' folktales:

✔ reflect information in their charts?

✔ show how the main characters grow or change?

✔ include lessons learned?

In this lesson, students write new folktales.

ADVICE FROM THE KNEE-HIGH MAN

In this activity, students explain what advice the knee-high man would have for us. Tell students to look carefully at the theme of the story to answer the question.

Sample Response:

Respect yourself and who you are. Don't try to change yourself to be like someone else. Use your brain when you need to solve problems.

A LESSON LEARNED

In this activity, students chart folktales that teach lessons they have learned. Students identify the Characters, Problem, and Outcome. Brainstorm problem areas and lessons as a whole class. Ideas might include self-esteem, respect, honesty, friendship, loyalty, and self-confidence.

Sample Response:

Characters	**Problem**	**Outcome**
Lion, bird	Having the courage to tell the truth.	In my folktale, the characters will learn that it is better to always tell the truth, no matter what happens. For one thing, people can count on it, and on you.

WRITE A FOLKTALE

In this activity, students write short folktales. Remind students to show how the characters grow or change because of the lessons learned.

Sample Response:

The Lion and the Bird

One day a bird was walking very slowly in the forest and met a lion. "Hello," said the lion. "You are a beautiful bird."

"I'm not a bird," said the bird. "I'm really a fantastic leopard."

"Really!" said the lion, impressed. "Well, I was going to offer you some dinner, but I can see that you can run faster than me. Good day." And he left.

The bird was tired and hungry. She wished she had told the lion the truth.

The next day the bird was limping along in the forest when she met an elephant....

(In the end the bird learns that if she had told the truth about being a bird in the beginning, she would have received friendship, help, and the respect of the other animals and herself.)

WRITING REMINDERS

As students complete their folktales, remind them to:

✔ Refer to their charts as they create their stories.

✔ Show how their characters grow, change, or learn something.

✔ Use their imaginations in creating the characters and dialogue.

3 Understanding Characters

Before Reading

FOCUS

Connecting to the experiences or feelings of characters helps us to understand them.

In the lesson, students see how remembering their own feelings or actions can help them understand characters in a story.

BUILDING BACKGROUND

Vocabulary Warm-up

Familiarize students with the vocabulary in this lesson with this **Matching Definitions** activity. Write the following words and definitions in two columns on the board. Ask students to match a word in the left column with its definition in the right column. For added practice, have students make up sentences for each word.

1. *notion*   a blank, empty look
2. *plantation*   gave up
3. *opportunity*   idea, opinion
4. *expressionless*   an agricultural farm worked by people who live there
5. *surrendered*   chance, occasion

Prereading Strategy

Build background for this selection with this **Anticipation Guide**. What do students already know about slavery issues and the Civil War? Present these sentences to get students thinking:

1. Agree   Disagree   The Civil War was fought about five years ago.
2. Agree   Disagree   Plantation owners were dependent on slaves to work on their plantations.
3. Agree   Disagree   Slaves were freed when the South lost the Civil War.

Reading the Selection

RESPONSE STRATEGY

In this story, students highlight parts of the story that remind them of experiences they've had.

   Sample Response:

(Highlighted) *None of them could remember ever hearing the bell in the afternoon.*

CRITICAL READING SKILL

In the Response Notes, students are asked to write what they feel as they read. Suggest that students write their comments as they highlight the text. That way they can write down their feelings immediately. (*Sample response: This reminds me of when the fire alarm went off in our school in the middle of math. It never rings in the afternoon. It was scary. It was a real fire.*)

REREADING

Have students read the story again, and this time focus on the ending. Ask students: Like the slaves who listened to Massa Brower that day, have you ever heard good news that left you unable to move or speak? Have them write about that experience in the Response Notes.

Writing

QUICK ASSESS

Do students' journal entries:

✓ make the experiences clear to readers?

✓ describe their feelings about the events?

✓ contain adequate details?

In this lesson, students write journal entries.

SARAH AND JAKE — WHEN THE BELL RINGS

In this activity, students describe the feelings of Sarah and Jake when they first hear the bell ring. Encourage students to think of a time when they might have felt like them. They might also *imagine* how they felt. Tell students that the more they can get inside each of the characters' skins, the richer their descriptions will be.

Sample Response:

(Sarah) Sarah wants to believe what Jake is saying is true, but she's scared. She has been disappointed before. She doesn't want to be disappointed again, especially about that. So instead, she teases Jake.

SARAH AND JAKE — AFTER HEARING THE NEWS

In this activity, students describe Sarah and Jake's feelings after they hear the news that they are free. How might their feelings change from what they were feeling earlier?

Sample Response:

(Jake) Jake felt his knees get all rubbery. He looked at Sarah. She was leaning against a railing. She had tears in her eyes. "Sarah," he said, "We are free. We're finally free." He sat down, head in hands, wondering what to do now. But Sarah was singing. She was leaping. She was dancing all over the place.

IMPORTANT NEWS

In this activity, students describe times when they heard important news. Encourage students to create word webs of the experiences. Who was there? What was the weather like? What were they wearing? What did they feel? What did they think? What did their bodies feel like? What did they say? Suggest that students take their time thinking back to the experiences and remembering as many details as possible.

Sample Response:

The day my grandma died the year I was six, it seemed like everything got very quiet. The wind didn't blow the wind chimes outside my window. Toby didn't bark. The only sound was the phone, which rang about every five minutes. I had on shorts and a T-shirt. I was going to go to my friend's house, but then I didn't. I couldn't cry. I couldn't do anything. No one in my family spoke. I think we were all busy missing my grandma terribly. I still do.

WRITING REMINDERS

As students complete their journal entries, remind them to:

✓ Think about their experiences and what they did, said, felt, and heard.

✓ Create word webs of the experiences to help organize their thoughts.

✓ Write about the events in detail.